CW01477036

Power and Partnership in Education

Who holds the power of decision making during the special needs assessment procedure? How important are the views of parents and the children themselves?

Recent legislation – the 1981 and 1993 Education Acts – has emphasized the need for parents to work as partners with professionals in the assessment of children's special educational needs. Derrick Armstrong explores that notion of partnership and subjects it to critical scrutiny. Drawing upon the comments of those directly involved, he describes the assessment process from both the parental and the professional standpoints, and discusses who holds the power throughout that process. The book looks in particular at the parent–professional relationship and the barriers that might inhibit the effectiveness of these partnerships. The child's viewpoint is equally important, and later chapters examine children's own accounts of the assessment procedure.

Power and Partnership in Education both praises the personal commitment shown by many professionals and raises serious questions about the role of professionals within the social institutions of the state, and for this reason may be seen as a controversial text. However, the issues raised cannot be disregarded and this book will be important for all those involved in the assessment process.

Derrick Armstrong is based at the University of Sheffield.

Power and Partnership in Education

Parents, Children and Special Educational Needs

Derrick Armstrong

ROUTLEDGE

London and New York

First published 1995
by Routledge
11 New Fetter Lane, London EC4P 4EE

Simultaneously published in the USA and Canada
by Routledge
29 West 35th Street, New York, NY 10001

© 1995 Derrick Armstrong

Typeset in Times by Michael Mepham, Frome, Somerset

Printed and bound in Great Britain by
Mackays of Chatham PLC, Chatham, Kent

British Library Cataloguing in Publication Data
A catalogue record for this book is available from the British
Library

Library of Congress Cataloguing in Publication Data
A catalogue record for this book has been requested

ISBN 0–415–08642–6 (hbk)
ISBN 0–415–08643–4 (pbk)

Contents

Tables

Acknowledgements

This book arises out of research undertaken in three local education authorities between 1989 and 1991 into the assessment of children identified as having emotional and behavioural difficulties (ebd) under the provisions of the 1981 Education Act. The research on which the author was employed as research associate was funded by the Economic and Social Research Council (Grant no. R 000 23 1393) and directed by David Galloway and Sally Tomlinson. The support of the Research Council is gratefully acknowledged. I am also especially grateful to David and Sally for allowing me so much freedom to develop my own interests during this research and for the immense support and encouragement they have always given me.

I would particularly like to thank Len Barton, Bob Burgess and Elizabeth Leo for their critical but very helpful comments on draft chapters of this book.

I would also like to thank Suzanne, Jennifer and Robert for their patience and support throughout this project, and my parents without whose faith it would never have been started.

Finally, but not least, I am grateful to the necessarily anonymous children, parents, teachers, psychologists, doctors, social workers and LEA officers who took part in the research.

Introduction

The aim of this book is to subject the concept of 'partnership' in special educational decision-making to critical scrutiny. Much has been written about partnership but, although some of this has been supportive of the principle and some critical of its practice, there have been few attempts to combine a systematic empirical analysis with a theoretical critique. It would be arrogant and probably a long way from the mark to suggest that this book represents a definitive account of the concept in these terms but in a more humble fashion I have attempted to move down this path. In doing so, it soon became clear that the book would be as much about power as it was about partnership.

The power to define the needs of others, which is implicit in the activity of professionals involved in the assessment of special educational needs, stands somewhat awkwardly in relation to the humanitarian principles frequently used by professionals in theorizing their own practice. Power necessarily stands in relation to something else. It exists as power over something or someone, and it is the dependency of this 'other' that conversely defines the limits of power. In this sense power is also dependent upon the unmet needs of those who lack power. Thus, power is only meaningful in so far as it creates the dependency of the powerless. This implies that there is a contradiction in the professional–client relationship in special education assessments between benevolence and control which the concept of 'partnership' does little to address. Essentially the contradiction arises because professionals have the power to select children whose needs will receive 'special' attention. Once identified as 'in need' these children relinquish or are deprived of the power to define their own interests legitimately in opposition to the political and social interests which have created their dependency. The inclusion of children and their families into this decision-making process through partnerships with professionals serves then to legitimize their dependency and therefore their lack of power.

Yet, the contradiction can only be partially understood in the simplistic terms of opposing interests. Its character lies in the fact that these conflicting aspects of assessment are so often combined within the same act. Thus, partnership appears to have the capacity to liberate parents and children by giving them access to decision-making machinery whilst at the same time controlling them through that very machinery. Similarly, professionals may also be disempowered by the procedures through which they exercise power, as where the use of the label 'special' by teachers leads to the removal of a troublesome child but at the same time threatens public perceptions of their professional competence. Inevitably the ambiguity which is a feature of professional contributions to partnership raises questions about the ambiguity of professionals' interests and roles, ambiguities which have been amplified in recent years as professionals working in education have increasingly faced the sharp end of government policies.

The 1981 Education Act made major changes to the procedures for identifying and assessing the educational needs of children who, prior to this legislation, had been classified according to categories of 'handicap' (Ministry of Education 1945). Following the recommendations of the Warnock Report (DES 1978), the 1981 Act purported to change the focus of assessment away from the identification of handicaps and towards the assessment of special educational needs. Henceforth, needs were to be understood in much broader terms as occurring within the context of an interrelationship between particular children and particular environments. In theory, at least, an assessment was now to be concerned with evaluating the appropriateness and quality of education received by a child experiencing difficulties rather than with deficits in the child's ability to benefit from particular forms of schooling.

In practice, there is widespread evidence that the child frequently continues to be the sole focus of the assessment procedures with the inevitable outcome that the child's needs are individualized as the 'problem' (see, for instance, Moses and Croll 1987). How professionals use such concepts as 'moderate learning difficulties', 'severe learning difficulties', 'emotional and behavioural difficulties', and so on, in their practice is an important area of interest. Similarly, it is of interest how such concepts come to have meaning for non-professionals (that is, children and their parents) involved in an assessment of special educational needs. One of the aims of this book is to explore parents' and children's experiences of the assessment procedures and how their understanding of the concept of special educational needs develops in the context of the professional–client interaction of the assessment process.

The 1981 Education Act states that in the assessment of children's special educational needs parents are to be partners with professionals working within a framework of multi-disciplinary co-operation. The enhanced status of parents within these procedures is reflected in the duty placed upon LEAs by the legislation to seek parental advice and to consult fully with them prior to decisions being taken. Furthermore, LEAs are obliged under the terms of the Act to make available to parents copies of any advice that has been sought to assist them in arriving at their decision about whether or not to provide a child with a statement of special educational needs. Necessarily, the information which parents receive must include the statutory reports of a psychologist, a doctor and the child's teacher. Additionally, parents have the right to make representations to the LEA in the form of 'parental advice' which, if provided, must also be given full consideration by the LEA and included as supplementary material to any statement of special educational needs which may subsequently be issued. The breadth of parental involvement in the decision-making process which is available to parents under the legislation appears to be so extensive that at first sight it is perhaps difficult to appreciate how parents come to feel so disempowered within and even by those procedures. Exploration of this apparent contradiction will be a central concern of the book.

Although the 1981 Act itself made no mention of the role and rights of children within the assessment procedures, the Department of Education and Science (DES 1983, 1989a) did state a clear view in its advice on the implementation of the Act that, where possible, the views of children should be sought and they should be encouraged to participate as partners in the assessment and decision-making procedures. The 1993 Education Act, in conjunction with a Code of Practice on the Identification and Assessment of Special Educational Needs (DFE 1994), has recently brought educational legislation into line with the 1989 Children Act in this respect by placing a duty on LEAs to seek the views of children for whom an assessment of special educational needs is being prepared. Despite this there is little evidence of professionals incorporating these principles into their practice.

AIMS AND METHOD OF THE RESEARCH

The research reported in this book started from a desire to understand the experience of assessment from the perspectives of those most significantly affected by it: children and their parents. The study examined the assessments of twenty-nine children in three LEAs who had been referred to the schools psychological service under the provisions of the 1981 Education Act because of their 'emotional and behavioural difficulties' (ebd). The children included were broadly representative in terms of social class, sex distribution and behaviour problems, as described at the time of referral, of children attending schools specializing in ebd. The main parts of each child's assessment were observed and each participant subsequently interviewed using semi-structured interviewing techniques. Retrospective interviews were held with a further eighteen children following their placement in either an off-site unit or residential special school specializing in the education of children with emotional and behavioural difficulties.

STRUCTURE OF THE BOOK

Chapters 1 to 3 are concerned with the contribution of parents to decision-making in respect of children with special educational needs. Chapter 1 reviews the fairly extensive literature on the participation of parents in the assessment of children's special educational needs. This discussion is located within the broader context of parental contributions to educational decision-making and includes a critical appraisal of both 'humanitarian' and 'consumerist' versions of the 'parents as partners' model. Chapter 2 describes key aspects of the 1981 Education Act assessment procedures from the perspective of parents whose children were identified as having emotional and behavioural difficulties. This chapter offers an overview of parental experiences and perspectives, and introduces some themes which are developed in subsequent chapters. In Chapter 3 the roles of professionals involved in assessments under the 1981 Act are examined, looking in particular at the parent–professional relationship and the barriers that may inhibit effective partnerships between parents and professionals. It is argued here that for some parents, their attempts to pursue particular outcomes by participating as 'partners' in the assessment procedures may actually contribute to their disempowerment. In consequence, parental participation may legitimize outcomes where an underlying and fundamental conflict is masked by an apparent parent–professional consensus. Yet, despite the view, well-established in the literature, that parents lack power in the assessment procedures, evidence is discussed which suggests that some parents do successfully negotiate what, from their point of view, are satisfactory outcomes.

Chapters 4 to 6 focus upon the experience and role of children in the assessment of emotional and behavioural difficulties. Chapter 4 looks at the fairly sparse literature dealing with the child's contribution to educational decision-making, Chapter 5 examines children's own accounts of the assessment process and Chapter 6 looks at the professional assessment of children identified as having emotional and behavioural difficulties. The 'clinical' practices of professionals carrying out assessments are examined and the effectiveness of these attempts at gaining access to the child's perspective is questioned. Consideration is given to ways in which interactions between children and professionals during the assessment contribute to the construction of a 'deviant' identity for the child. Case-study data are examined which suggests that children, as well as professionals and parents, use strategies during the assessment procedure in an attempt to negotiate an outcome, or at least a consensus about their needs, that is acceptable to them. It is argued that these strategies may on occasions be successful but that they may also lead to the contradictory outcome of reinforcing the very perspectives which they oppose. Often professionals are unaware of children's own perspectives regarding the difficulties they encounter in their schooling. This happens because those children rarely have meaningful opportunities for contributing to the assessment on an equal footing with adult participants. In these circumstances the rhetoric of partnership between professionals and children can reinforce the child's vulnerability and legitimize the power of adults.

Chapter 7 returns to the theme of professional identities and considers how negotiations about the needs of professionals operate to conceptualize children's needs in particular ways. The concept of 'deprofessionalization' developed in the literature on teachers and teaching is introduced. Building on this, it is argued that from the perspective of teachers the identification of behaviour as 'disturbed' may in particular cases serve to reconstruct the teacher's work with 'normal' children as 'skilful'. The effect of the decision to carry out an assessment on children's subsequent perception of their own needs is considered. Negotiations over professional roles are identified as central to the assessment of children labelled as having special educational needs. It is argued that although the ideal of partnership between professionals and their clients is strongly influenced by genuine concerns about identifying and meeting children's needs, in practice these procedures may actually focus upon negotiations over areas of professional responsibility and control in the context of decision-making about the management of resources. This is discussed within the broader context of the changing role of professionals within the modern state. Finally, in Chapter 8, some of the theoretical, policy and professional implications of the analysis put forward in this book are considered.

There is much in this book which is critical of professional practice with regard to the assessment of special educational needs but it is not written from a perspective which condemns professionals out of hand. The personal commitment shown by teachers, psychologists, doctors and other professionals involved in this research towards seeking solutions to problems, in circumstances which were often very difficult and sometimes traumatic, can only be admired. In writing this book I have not intended to undermine such work, but to raise serious questions about the role of professionals within the social institutions of the state. More than anything my aim has been to attack the notion that professionals can remain neutral in respect of conflicts of interest between the different social classes and groupings that constitute society. No doubt there will be many who will disagree with the arguments advanced in this book, and that is as it should be, but I would contend that these issues cannot be disregarded without implicitly welding one's professional practice to the interests of the powerful in opposition to the powerless.

Chapter 1

Parents as partners in the assessment of special educational needs

The involvement of parents in the formal education of their children in the United Kingdom stands today at the crossroads between two ideologically conflicting conceptions of its purpose. On the one hand, there is the view, encapsulated in the social welfare policies which were in ascendance during the period of post-war reform, that the state in partnership with its citizenry can and should work towards improving the conditions of people's lives, especially for those who are disadvantaged. On the other hand, there is the view, espoused by the neo-liberal 'new right', that a system of state welfare stifles the independence and self-reliance of individuals, the family and local communities. From the former perspective, parent–professional partnership in education was seen as central to achieving the desired improvements for future generations. The neo-liberal perspective, by contrast, with its origins in the demise of the post-war economic miracle, has taken a much more cautious view of the 'benefits', of partnership, radically confronting what it sees as the professional self-interest of a 'left-wing', interventionist bureaucracy (Cox *et al.* 1986).

In this chapter these differing attitudes towards the role of parents in educational decision-making are examined. The contribution of parents within the procedures for assessing children with special educational needs is considered in detail, with particular reference to the Warnock Report (DES 1978) and the 1981 and 1993 Education Acts. Whereas the 1980 and 1986 Education Acts and, more especially, the 1988 Education Reform Act made widespread and fundamental changes to the organization and control of the education system in this country, the pattern of reform in special education has, to date, been less affected by the thinking of the new right. Although local management of special schools has been introduced and, at the time of writing, the first special school in the country is about to be awarded grant-maintained status, the principles of social welfarism implicit in the main legislation concerning the assessment and resourcing of children with special educational needs (the 1981 Education Act) have recently been reaffirmed in the 1993 Education Act. Perhaps this is because children with special needs are seen as especially vulnerable and therefore more dependent upon the goodwill of the community in the form of a state-supported safety net. None the less, it would be quite wrong to think that the absence of market forces legislation relating to the assessment of special educational needs suggests that these different philosophies are compatible. The circumstances in which special needs legislation is being implemented in the 1990s are very different from those of the late 1970s when the principles underlying this legislation were formulated. This difference has increasingly become a source of tension between professionals and parents as gaps appear between their respective goals and strategies for achieving these goals. Whilst professionals frequently find themselves in the role of gatekeeper to declining resources in the context of ever-growing demand, there is evidence that the parents of some children with special educational needs, particularly those who are most articulate in advancing their interests through well-organized pressure groups, are increasingly willing to challenge professional judgements through the courts. As will be argued here, the pressures on resources both from within and from outside the education system, together with the contradictions implicit in professional roles, help to explain some of the conflict that occurs between parents and professionals. Yet, in this chapter it is also argued that the disempowerment of parents within the assessment system does not stem simply from conflicts between the ideology of conception and the ideology of implementation. Contradictions within the model of parent–professional partnership espoused by Warnock and the 1981 and 1993 Acts are identified as likely to reduce the power of parents in the decision-making process. This critique will suggest that the inadequacy of thinking about the relationship between 'power' and 'needs' is a central weakness of the partnership model.

POST-WAR EDUCATIONAL REFORM AND A NEW AGE OF PARTNERSHIP

The years following the end of the Second World War were characterized by social reform as aspirations arising from a new world order were fuelled by increasing prosperity and technological advance. Whereas the years preceding the war had been ones of industrial decline, unemployment and wastage of talent, in the new era rapid economic growth and the revolution in production processes made demands on the education system that coincided with and added to the momentum of change in society. A new vision of the contribution of education to social development and prosperity began with the 1944 Education Act and was followed by a flurry of research activity and government reports. Education was seen as the key to change in society, by reformers who saw it as the catalyst and vehicle for realizing their aspirations for the masses, and by those at the forefront of the new economic revival who saw it as the means of preparing a skilled and motivated work-force.

These changes in British society were mirrored in debates taking place in the political and social science literature of the time. The political and economic stability which characterized early post-war Britain was reflected in claims that affluence and social mobility were eroding the traditional class system (Abrams and Rose 1960). However, Goldthorpe *et al.* (1968), who investigated the so-called *embourgeoisement* of the working class did not find any convincing evidence of the working class being assimilated into the middle class. Given the evidence of increased working-class affluence, it was suggested by some commentators that it was actually the cultural traditions of the working classes rather than any inherent imperfections in the system that were the main barriers preventing social mobility based on merit. A sophisticated form of this argument is to be found, for instance, in Bernstein's (1962) claim that the linguistic deprivation of working-class children meant that they did not command the complex grammatical forms which would give them access to power.

Fraser (1959), in a study of schoolchildren in Aberdeen, found home environment to be a factor more closely associated with progress in school than IQ. Jackson and Marsden's (1962) study of working-class children attending grammar schools illustrated the difficulties encountered by such children as they sought to come to terms with the cultural and value differences between middle-class schools and working-class families. In a longitudinal study of more than 5,000 children born in 1946 and followed from birth to adolescence, Douglas (1964) found children from manual working-class backgrounds to be more prone to the negative effects of their social and physical environment, particularly during their junior school years. The test performances of these children tended to decline as they progressed through school. However, Douglas noted that, where a great interest was taken in the progress of these children at school by their parents, test performances showed improvement. Another national research project, this time carried out on behalf of the Plowden Committee (CACE 1967), involving interviews with more than 3,000 parents about their attitudes towards education, provided further evidence of the important link between parental attitudes and attainment.

The growing weight of evidence which identified parental attitudes, linked to disadvantaged social background, as the most significant factor having a negative effect upon educational progress was encapsulated in the recommendations of the Plowden Report into primary education (CACE 1967). This Report concluded that the influence of background factors such as living conditions and parental attitudes were crucial to children's educational prospects and, therefore, that where negative and ill-informed attitudes persisted concerted efforts must be made to persuade parents of the value of education for their children. This, it was argued, could be achieved by encouraging the involvement of parents in their children's education through co-operation and partnership with teachers. Paragraph 151 of the Report argues that the principle

> that special need calls for special help, should be given a new cutting edge. We ask for 'positive discrimination' in favour of such schools and the children in them, going well beyond an attempt to equalise resources. Schools in deprived areas should be given priority in many respects. . . . The justification is that the homes and neighbourhoods from which many of their children come provide little support or stimulus for learning. The schools must provide a compensating environment.

The Plowden Report, therefore, advanced the new and highly proactive principle of compensatory intervention. This was made concrete by a recommendation for Educational Priority Areas to be designated for the allocation of additional resources. Three principles underpinned positive discrimination in the use of resources.

First, there was a belief that it was the duty of the state to intervene in order to maximize opportunities for all its citizenry. Acceptance of this belief at that time reflected what is a very simple but basic truth about social welfare principles; namely, that they are more likely to influence policy during times of economic growth. Decisions about resource allocation are inevitably concerned with the prioritization of needs and interests. The availability of resources does not of itself determine resource allocation because a prior decision is always made about the level of resource that it is ethically and/or politically desirable to make available. Yet, addressing the problem of social disadvantage at times of economic expansion is a benevolence that can be afforded both economically and politically because it threatens neither wealth creation nor political stability. Within a climate of economic recession, however, welfare programmes are more likely to be sacrificed precisely when they are most needed. Social reform becomes threatening, not simply because welfare programmes are expensive or 'uneconomic' but also because they raise hopes that the system cannot or will not meet. In consequence, needs become individualized as social responsibility is rejected.

The second principle that underpinned the Plowden Report's support for compensatory education was that of 'partnership' between parents and professionals. In working with parents of educationally disadvantaged children the Plowden Report envisaged professionals exercising their specialist knowledge on behalf, and in support, of the best interests of children and their families. The rhetoric of partnership was enthusiastically embraced as symbolic of the fresh wind of change sweeping through society, but the ideology of partnership was always derived more from belief in a new professionalism based upon the rational application of knowledge than from any principle of participatory democracy. In so far as the inadequacies of working-class family and community life were held responsible (whatever the underlying causes) for the educational deprivation from which many children suffered, the idea of partnership was centrally concerned with *improving* the labouring classes to make them fit for democracy. It was not concerned with transferring power directly to those whose lives up to that time had been blighted by the injustices of an exclusive and discriminatory system of education. The partnership demanded of parents by compensatory education required their acceptance of the disinterested, humanitarian rationalism of professional judgements.

Some years later Kirp was to describe the model of professionalism based on this benevolent humanitarianism as one which 'contemplates professionals and administrators working on behalf of an ever-expanding clientele towards an agreed common goal' (1983: 83).

However, once again the economic context in which parent–professional partnership occurs is highly relevant. Whereas this model may match the demands placed on professionals during periods of economic growth and social reform, it is a model that is subject to increasing tensions during periods of social and economic upheaval and dislocation. The real significance of partnerships between professionals and parents may lie not in the incorporation of parents into decision-making processes but rather in the incorporation of educational professionals into the state bureaucracy.

A third principle, highly significant for the development of a programme of compensatory education, was the rejection in the Plowden Report of the idea that educational 'handicap' arises from individual deficits. This view, in particular, was to have important consequences for the future of special education in Britain. For Plowden, the absence of opportunities was understood in terms of deficits within working-class families and communities. This view lacked the depth of analysis which would have enabled consideration of the way in which social institutions, including the education system, themselves create and reinforce the social and economic disadvantages which can undermine the pursuit of learning and educational success. None the less, it was an analysis which differed significantly from earlier (and later) analyses of needs in that it acknowledged that there should be a collective responsibility towards those individuals who experienced learning difficulties in their education.

Criticisms of the Plowden Report are not confined to the recent assaults of the new right. Acland (1980), for instance, has argued that research was used both sparingly and selectively to justify the ideological position adopted by the Plowden Committee. It placed an emphasis upon education as a pathway for individual advancement and social mobility which is at least questionable and which ignores the wider social and economic context of deprivation and its reproduction. Moreover, its assumptions about professional judgement disregard the way in which professional interests may be advanced through the creation of 'needy' client groups who are subsequently disenfranchised on the grounds that they lack the knowledge to exercise power rationally. Yet without doubt, the Plowden Report represented a milestone in educational thinking and one which continued to influence policy making in the United Kingdom right up to the emergence of neo-liberalism in the 1980s. As will be argued in the following section, it also contained ideas which laid the basis for the fundamental reappraisal of the system of special education subsequently undertaken by the Warnock Committee (DES 1978).

PARENT–PROFESSIONAL PARTNERSHIP IN SPECIAL EDUCATION

It is perhaps not surprising that the system of special education in Britain, located as it was on the fringes and directly involving the interests of a comparatively small section of the population, lagged behind the changes taking place within the mainstream of the system. The 1944 Education Act had introduced new procedures under which local authorities were made responsible for the provision of special education for handicapped pupils. Yet the concept of 'need' remained tied to a view of handicap as something intrinsic to individuals and focused towards providing education within limits defined by the nature of particular disabilities. This definition of needs as the product of individual handicap had significant implications for the role of parents in decision-making interactions with professionals.

Educational decision-making in respect of the handicapped child was subordinated to medical decision-making. Therefore, the criteria governing decisions about the education of the handicapped child were medical criteria related to treatment and generally outside the domain of most parents' expertise. Furthermore, there was an assumption inherent in the concept of handicap that the *condition* necessarily disables the child in his or her relation to the world. Whilst needs were conceptualized as arising from disablement, rather than created by the nature of social interactions directly and indirectly involving the child, it followed that responses to the child would be defined by the child's disability rather than by educational goals such as equal opportunity, inclusiveness, transformation of potentiality into actuality and so on, all of which are areas of legitimate concern to parents and which, as value positions, are not determinable by expertise. Thus, the disempowerment experienced by parents had its origins in the conceptualization of children's disabilities which dominated professional practice at that time.

The Handicapped Pupils and School Health Regulations (Ministry of Education 1945) identified eleven categories of handicapped pupil (later amended to ten – Ministry of Education 1959). A child could be 'ascertained' by a school medical officer as suffering from a condition described by one of these categories of 'disability of mind or body'. Following 'ascertainment' the child would be placed in a special school, yet, as Galloway and Goodwin (1979) have argued, the 1944 Act and subsequent regulations only empowered the authority to request a formal certificate of ascertainment. They did not compel it to do so when it wished to place a child in a special school. Section 34 of the 1944 Education Act was explicit in stating that formal ascertainment was only needed when an LEA wished to impose attendance at a special school against parental wishes. None the less, local authorities very often ascertained all children placed in special schools.

> This served to emphasise the separate nature of special education, with an implicit assumption that 'special' education could only be provided in schools or classes recognised by the DES as efficient for the education of children with a particular category of handicap. The formality helped to ensure that transfer from special schools to the mainstream was a rare event.
>
> (Galloway 1985a: 29)

Thus, these procedures served to reinforce the division between ordinary and mainstream schools and in doing so emphasized the stigma of special education.

Confusion about the ascertainment procedures resulted in parents being deprived of rights they had been given under the 1944 Education Act. In addition, parents were brought into a formal relationship with professionals through the ascertainment procedures at a time when inter-professional conflict over domains of responsibility for the assessment of special education needs was becoming increasingly acute. This conflict was a factor contributing to the sense of powerlessness parents experienced as interests other than the child's became a focal point of the assessment (Tomlinson 1982).

In the period leading up to the 1981 Education Act evidence was mounting of the dissatisfaction parents felt with the role allotted to them by LEAs and professionals. The self-reports of parents on this theme are many (see, for example, Booth and Statham 1982; Hannam 1975). These reports were scathing not only about the limited contribution parents were allowed to make to decisions affecting their children but also publicized how the paternalistic interventions of professionals at the early stages of decision-making could have long-term effects on the ability and willingness of parents to take on board their responsibilities towards their children in the future.

Tomlinson (1981), in a study of the assessment of forty children, identified as 'educationally subnormal' found that on the whole parents did not feel themselves to have been sufficiently informed by their LEAs of the reasons for the decisions that had been taken. There was a widespread perception on the part of these parents that little had been offered by way of an explanation of their children's needs or of the procedures by which these needs had been assessed. In Tomlinson's view this reflected the absence of any machinery in the assessment procedure which would place parents on an equal footing with professionals. Assessments tended to be based on assumptions that were rarely made explicit by the professionals. These were derived from professionals' perceptions of their own professional roles and interests rather than from any 'objective' assessment of the child's needs.

This was described very graphically by Dyson (1986) in research which examined the assessments of twenty children who had been identified as severely educationally subnormal in 1982 and 1983 (prior to the implementation of the 1981 Education Act). His analysis of the files of the professionals conducting these assessments led him to conclude that the secrecy of the procedures contributed to 'the oppression of the clients'. Moreover, he argued that the failure to allow parents access to information that was freely transferred between professionals served to legitimize the professionals' role in the procedures rather than contributing anything that might benefit the interests of the child.

Whilst children with special educational needs were seen as different from other children by virtue of their disabilities, decisions about these children were framed in terms of responses to the individual disability rather than in terms of a wider context of equal opportunities for all. This contrasts sharply with the view developed in the Plowden Report, where needs were understood as arising from social and environmental deficits with the implication that it is the role of the education system to compensate for the disabling effects of environmental factors so that the child's potential can be maximized. The philosophy of compensatory education was more accurately reflected in the later Warnock Report (DES 1978), which rejected a conceptualization of needs in terms of individual disabilities, preferring to approach the concept of needs from the standpoint of the educational interventions necessary for improving the quality of learning opportunity. For Warnock, needs were seen as occurring along a continuum rather than expressing *qualitative* differences. This carried the implication, in theory at least, that the decision-making process for the child with special needs should be no different from that relating to any other child.

Mounting pressure for reform, therefore, can be seen as emanating on the one hand from inconsistencies between the new educational philosophy of the Plowden Report and the old medical model of special needs implicit in the 1944 Education Act; and, on the other, from the demands of parents for reform of the procedures surrounding special educational assessments and placements. However, a third source of pressure for reform arose from the long running inter-professional dispute over which professional group should have primary responsibility for the identification of special educational needs.

Under the 1945 and 1959 regulations (Ministry of Education 1945, 1959) governing the assessment procedures for handicapped children primary responsibility for the assessment was placed with the medical officers employed by the local health authority. Yet increasingly, from the turn of the century onwards, the claim of the medical profession exclusively to possess specialized knowledge and skills appropriate to the assessment of children's educational needs was being contested. This was particularly so in relation to the categories of educational subnormality and maladjustment where new procedures for mental testing were being developed by the fledgling profession of educational psychology (Tomlinson 1981).

Galloway and Goodwin (1987) have pointed out that the government circular 2/75 (DES 1975) which recommended that a summary of educational, medical and psychological reports be prepared for the education administration by an experienced educational psychologist not only anticipated the 1981 Act but actually placed psychologists in a stronger position in relation to their medical colleagues than was the case after 1981. Yet Tomlinson's (1981) study indicated that, despite circular 2/75, in practice there remained wide variations in the distribution of power between different professional groups from one local authority to another. Moreover, according to Tomlinson, these inter-professional rivalries and conflicts were themselves significant in contributing to the particular form of label attached to disadvantaged groups and individuals. Indeed, the disadvantage itself might be a consequence of inter-professional conflict. Such conflict, she argued, focused upon 'the status of professional judgements and the power implicit in these judgements which legitimizes the complex procedures which make the categorisation an objective reality' (Tomlinson 1981: 11). According to Tomlinson, the marginalization of parents in the decision-making process was a direct consequence of such conflicts over the status and power of professional groups in their relation to one another.

THE WARNOCK REPORT

The Warnock Report (DES 1978) had wide-ranging significance for subsequent special educational policy and practice. One area in which the Report laid the foundations for a new approach was in relation to parental involvement in special education assessments. The Report finally gave official legitimacy to the principle of parent–professional partnership in special education. The challenge for professionals was subsequently seen to be one of developing a model of multi-professional intervention that could also facilitate the contribution of parents as partners. That there are significant difficulties involved in meeting this challenge is something that is generally acknowledged. For example, if partnership is to be effective parents must have the same rights of access as professionals to information that is used in decision-making about their children's needs. Yet Mittler and Mittler (1982) have shown how the 'disclosure' of information by professionals to parents may serve to reinforce a sense of disempowerment on the part of parents. Whereas the concept of 'partnership' emphasizes the sharing of power as well as expertise, in practice the parent–professional relationship may be primarily built upon a model of 'involvement' containing an implicit assumption of professional expertise and control. In so far as the Warnock Report did not concern itself with these subtleties its recommendations may be seen as rather naïve or even, if one cares to see it that way, as a disingenuous attempt to maintain the subordinate role of parents *vis-à-vis* that of professionals. However, its recommendations for parental involvement must be seen within the overall context of an attempt to construct a more rational framework for identifying and dealing with children with special educational needs.

Central to this rationalistic view was the creation of a multi-disciplinary framework for assessment within which parents would be active participants. This multi-disciplinary approach would provide a forum for resolving conflict based upon recognition of the individual expertise of all participants and of the particular value of each contribution to the building of a holistic picture of the child's needs. Here the Warnock Report was reiterating the view expressed earlier in the Court Report (Department of Health and Social Security 1976) that to 'disentangle the strands [that make up a child's needs] is beyond any single expertise' (para. 10: 39). The Warnock Report, therefore, sought to encourage co-operation amongst professionals as well as between professionals and parents.

Although there is a popular perception of the Warnock Report as being a charter of parents' rights, a different and more critical view of its recommendations on parental involvement has been put forward by Galloway and Goodwin, who argued that the composition of the committee 'reflected the prevalent view that decisions on special education were best left to professionals. Consumers, in the form of parents or young people, could not be expected to know what was best for their children' (1987: 13).

A similar view was put forward by Kirp (1983), who maintained that the Warnock Report was underpinned by a belief in professional benevolence based upon the professional's role as 'expert'. Despite its rhetoric about partnerships with parents, the principal concern of the Report is that of elaborating a model of good professional practice founded upon a belief in disinterested rationality as the basis of professionalism. In arguing against the exclusion of parents from aspects of the assessment process its arguments were not based upon a theory of parental rights but rather on the view that parents had special knowledge of their children and without access to this knowledge professionals could not make informed judgements concerning children's needs and how these should be met.

In case there might have been any confusion about what was actually being advocated under the banner of 'parents as partners' in the Warnock Report, the Report's author subsequently took the opportunity to clarify the issue in an article published in the *Listener*:

in educational matters, parents cannot be equals to teachers if teachers
are to be regarded as true professionals. Even though educating a child
is a joint enterprise involving both home and school, parents should
realise that they cannot have the last word. It is a question of collaboration not partnership.

(Warnock 1985: 12)

As Warnock argued in this article, it may be the case that parents'
knowledge of their child can help the teacher to work more effectively
with the child at school but this will only be so if the teacher is willing to
acknowledge parents' expert knowledge. Yet, the reverse is also true.
Partnership implies (1) mutual respect; (2) complementary expertise; (3)
willingness to learn from each other. It does not imply that the status of
parents is any less than that of teachers in educational decision-making.
By suggesting that professionals have some superior expertise which
gives them the authority to override the views of parents Warnock's
argument is both arrogant and sloppy.

THE 1981 AND 1993 EDUCATION ACTS

Section 1(1) of the 1981 Education Act refers to a child as having special
educational needs 'if he has a learning difficulty which calls for special
educational provision to be made for him'. This will be the case where he
or she 'has a significantly greater difficulty in learning than the majority
of children of his age; [or] he has a disability which either prevents or
hinders him from making use of educational facilities of a kind generally
provided in schools'.

According to Oliver (1988), this definition in practice perpetuates a
within-child model by focusing upon how the child's needs can be met
within the context of schooling rather than upon how those needs are
created by those situations (including the interactions that take place
within them). Galloway and Goodwin (1987) have similarly argued that
reference to a child's needs may actually refer to something the teacher
wants to be provided on the child's behalf. Moreover, they claim that
concern over the progress or behaviour of an individual child 'may be little
more than a *post hoc* rationalization of the teacher's absolutely reasonable
concern about the progress of other children' (Galloway and Goodwin
1987: 17).

Fulcher (1989) has criticized the Act for its retention of a 'discourse
on disability'. She argues that the 1981 Act

defines special education as provision; in the context of a state apparatus this means resources in general. . . . The Act establishes a generalist discourse and provides a basis for negotiating over and focusing on, resources rather than examining the educational and social context in which particular 'needs' might emerge.

(Fulcher 1989: 167)

Whilst the definition of 'needs' in any given situation may arise from negotiations taking place between people with differing and, sometimes, conflicting interests (those of teachers, parents, other pupils, the LEA and the LEA's professional advisers, for example), the Act ignores the role of conflicting interests in the construction of individual needs, focusing solely upon the needs of the child once they have been identified as present. Consequently, the child's needs become the focal point for parallel negotiations between all interested parties over the allocation of resources. Yet this may inhibit the development of a theoretical framework within which the interplay of interests and needs can be examined (Armstrong and Galloway 1992a). The development of an appropriate framework revolves around two central questions: 'Whose needs are defined?' and 'Who has the power to define needs?' The 1981 Education Act, based as it is upon a premise of humanitarian benevolence, treats these questions as unproblematic.

The Warnock Report did exercise considerable influence over the role eventually given to parents by subsequent legislation on special education. The 1981 Education Act placed a wide range of requirements on LEAs aimed at maximizing the participation of parents and the benefits to the child of parent–professional partnership. These have subsequently been restated and strengthened in the 1993 Education Act. Thus, the 1993 Act, Section 167, stipulates that

> Before making an assessment, the LEA must write to the child's parent to explain their proposal. The LEA must also inform the parents of the procedure to be followed in making an assessment; of the name of the officer of the authority from whom further information may be obtained; and of their right to make representations and submit written evidence within a given time limit, which must not be less than twenty-nine days.

Sections 172 and 173 of the 1993 Act restate the right given to parents under Section 9(1) of the 1981 Education Act to request that an assessment be carried out by the LEA, which the latter must undertake unless an assessment has previously been carried out within the last six months or there are good grounds for considering an assessment to be unnecessary.

Schedule 10, paragraph 2, regulations 12 and 13 of the 1993 Act requires the LEA to submit a draft statement to parents specifying the proposals they wish to make for meeting a child's special educational needs where such needs have been identified or alternatively to inform parents of the decision not to issue a statement and of their right of appeal against this decision. A proposed statement must be accompanied by copies of the professional, parental and any other advice which the LEA has used in formulating its recommendations. The 1981 Education Act (Section 8) established local appeals committees which had the power to recommend to LEAs that they reconsider their decision in a case. These committees did not have the power to overrule LEA decisions although the 1993 Education Act has now created a new appeals framework of tribunals which does have this power.

It remains to be seen whether the 1993 Education Act will make any significant improvements to the position of parents. There is clear evidence, some of which will be reviewed in the following section, that parents have become increasingly disillusioned with the procedures for assessing children's special educational needs introduced by the 1981 Education Act. In part this has arisen because these procedures have been widely seen as primarily a bureaucratic gateway through which both teachers and parents must pass to obtain additional resources for children whose needs have been identified as special. They have less commonly been seen as providing a genuine framework for actually identifying those needs. Once again, the Code of Practice on the Identification and Assessment of Special Educational Needs (DFE 1994) goes some way towards providing this framework, but the extent to which these procedures will be 'workable' without the infusion of resources to schools is as yet unclear. In addition, the introduction of an appeals system with statutory powers may provide checks and balances within the system which will promote greater equity in decision-making. However, as with the Code of Practice, there are already doubts about the viability and effectiveness of the tribunal system. For the parents of children increasingly marginalized by social and economic pressures upon resources, the tribunal system may become just another bureaucratic hurdle that stands in the way of equal opportunities.

PARENT–PROFESSIONAL PARTNERSHIP AND THE ASSESSMENT OF CHILDREN WITH SPECIAL EDUCATIONAL NEEDS: A REVIEW OF RECENT EVIDENCE

The evidence of parental involvement in special educational decision-making is far from encouraging for advocates of the partnership model of assessment. Swann found that where parents had contributed to placement decisions this had generally been the result of their willingness to 'accept partnership on their opposite partner's terms' (1984: 10). Subsequent research by Goacher *et al.* (1988) in England and by Riddell *et al.* (1990) in Scotland has documented the continuing subordination of parental contributions to the interests of LEA bureaucracies. Only two years after the 1981 Education Act was fully implemented Sharron (1985: 20) argued that it was already clear that

> Any shift the 1981 Education Act may have been expected to make in the balance of power between parents and local authorities has clearly been frustrated by those LEAs who have manipulated the flow of information and undermined parents' negotiating powers.

Similar claims were made by Wright (1989), based on his experience of advising parents in his role as administrator for the Independent Panel of Special Educational Advisers. Indeed, the testimonies of parents continue to mirror many of the complaints that led to the enactment of the 1981 Education Act. The House of Commons Select Committee report on the implementation of the 1981 Act (House of Commons 1987) noted that evidence suggested parents remained unclear and ill-informed about the assessment procedures and special educational provision in general. The committee observed that the contribution of parents to the assessment was still likely to be ignored in practice where it differed from the advice of the professionals. Chaudhury (1986) and Rehal (1989) have each reported research indicating that parents of children in ethnic minority communities may suffer particular disadvantages in their relationships with professionals during the course of assessments under the 1981 Act.

Goacher *et al.*'s (1988) survey of the implementation of the 1981 Act in all English local authorities found evidence of widespread dissatisfaction on the part of parents with the level of involvement in the assessment procedures they perceived themselves as having. Moreover, complaints were common in relation to the poor quality and quantity of information parents alleged they had received from professionals and LEAs during their children's assessments. Attention was drawn by these authors to the wide diversity of policy and practice across different local authorities and the frequent lack of clear policy formulations within LEAs. An absence of clear policy created difficulties for parents, leaving them unclear about what to expect from an assessment of their children's special educational needs.

Parents may themselves be perceived by professionals as directly responsible for the child's problems. Where this occurs (both where such a perception is justified and where it is not), possibilities for developing genuine partnership between professionals and parents may be seriously impeded. Moses and Croll (1987) have argued that the heavy emphasis within social science on the importance of children's social circumstances and parental background in accounting for educational success and failure may, in part, account for teachers holding parents responsible for the educational difficulties of their children. As they suggest, 'If such views are widely held they will probably not provide a good basis for an effective partnership' (Moses and Croll 1987: 78).

That this is the case is suggested by research reported by Croll and Moses (1985), which found teachers to have a repertoire of explanations for children's difficulties which centre on the psychological characteristics of the child and social characteristics of homes and parents but which do not acknowledge any contribution that schools and teachers may themselves make to children's problems.

Swann (1987) has maintained that the notion of a partnership between parents and professionals is only viable where goals are shared. Even then partnership has little to do with the power or rights of parents. According to Swann, the doctrine of 'parents as partners' has 'rather more to do with recruiting parents as resources in the education of their children, pursuing goals defined by professionals' (1987: 193).

The assumption of shared goals, however, is a dubious one; where conflict between parents and professionals occurs the 1981 Education Act provides no mechanisms to facilitate the exercise of parental power. Swann (1987) argues that the main reason why parents lack power in this situation is that the assessment is not concerned with the child's curriculum needs so much as with the selective distribution of special education resources. Whilst this is so, the ability of parents to participate in the assessment process on an equal footing with professionals is dependent upon an open-ended access to resources. Adequate resourcing of the 1981 Act was never forthcoming, yet, once 'special educational needs' were defined in terms of the additional resources that ought to be made available, professionals were thrust into the role of gatekeepers and the possibility of genuine partnerships with parents was undermined.

From the evidence reviewed here two points may be seen as emerging. First, the absence of clear and consistent policy regarding implementation of the 1981 Act at both national and local levels means that the availability of resources may become the arbiter of decisions about children's needs. Second, the difficulties parents appear to have in exercising their rights under the 1981 Act suggests that the failure of the legislation to address the relationship between 'rights' and the power required to exercise those rights is a significant omission. Both these considerations could lead to inconsistencies in decision-making, reflecting responses to short-term pressures and the demands and influence of individuals and interest groups whose status, access to information and ability to negotiate other participants' perceptions of the problem, gives them unequal power within the assessment process.

MARKETS, RESOURCES AND NEEDS

Looking back from our own time in the mid-1990s, the Warnock Report may appear to have been an anachronism, even before it was published. The fact that it was commissioned by Margaret Thatcher, the incumbent Secretary of State for Education in 1974, is not without irony. Post-war optimism about the potential of education for engineering social reform had already begun to splutter, even before James Callaghan's (1976) call for a Great Debate challenged belief in a society guided by the rationality of professional technocracy and benevolence. By 1981 a new era had already begun in which much of the responsibility for Britain's alleged lack of industrial competitiveness was laid squarely at the door of those whose power was embedded in the post-war consensus; that is, the professional and administrative bureaucracies of the state itself.

The professional ethic of service came under increasing pressure during the 1980s and 1990s as the agenda for reform in education shifted away from that set by the liberal theories of consensus which had underpinned the philosophy of the Warnock Report. These were now replaced by a new orthodoxy of consumer-driven market forces (Cox *et al.* 1986; White 1988). The reforms of the new regime have struck at the heart of teachers' professional autonomy.

The devolution of resources from LEAs to schools has extended control over certain aspects of financial planning to a new managerial bureaucracy within schools, but it has also had the consequence of centralizing power over policy-making in the hands of the DFE and the Treasury. Whilst the ethos of teacher professionalism in LEAs was often equal in importance, if not greater, to the political ideologies of elected members, thus giving teachers direct access to policy-making mechanisms which counterbalanced government policy, the downgrading of LEAs has centralized both political and bureaucratic control over professional services in education.

The centralization of control over education has also created external pressures on schools and teachers to adopt pupil selection and financial policies that maximize their competitiveness in the market-place. The policy of government has been to make the delivery of professional services subject to the discipline of the market-place, with consumer (parental) choice becoming the arbiter of quality. Yet research on parental choice in education suggests that it is the middle and professional classes who are most likely to be in a position to exercise genuine choice over the schooling of their children (Adler *et al.* 1989; Echols *et al.* 1990; Stillman and Maychell 1986). Paquette (1991: 74) puts it as follows: 'The conservative doctrine of freedom of choice becomes, in education, the freedom of parents who can afford to choose among schools, but never the freedom of all parents and students to choose any learning they wish.'

In the jargon of educational markets it has become fashionable for schools to be referred to as 'providers' and parents as 'consumers' or 'purchasers', but this reflects a very unidimensional understanding of the market-place. Schools not only provide educational services but also consume through transformation of their raw materials. Likewise, for parents education can be an investment in the future of their children, perpetuating or enhancing the social capital of the family. Schools are provided with their raw materials by parents and hence are in competition not just for good results but for 'good' intakes. In this market-place children inevitably become commodities to which value is attached at different stages of the process of production. Thus, the concept of a 'market' in educational services may create some limited choices for those who have the social and economic power to make choices, but this can only be at the expense of those who lack that power.

However, research in Scotland by Echols *et al.* (1990) found no evidence of the principle of parental choice which underpins the policy of 'open enrolment' (introduced in Scotland in 1981) leading to improvements in educational standards. There was evidence of choice leading to the ghettoization of some schools as middle-class parents were encouraged to identify successful schools on the criterion of social respectability defined by pupil intake. Maintaining and improving pupil numbers will in large part be dependent upon a school's appeal to this small but influential section of the population. Schools which are unattractive to the parents of these children are in the future increasingly unlikely to benefit from the changes in school funding that are being introduced.

In these circumstances teachers may find themselves under pressure to divert resources away from children with special educational needs (unless those resources are protected by a statement) towards those whose success is likely to enhance the academic reputation of the school. Moreover, the very presence of large numbers of children with special needs, particularly where those needs arise from learning and/or behaviour difficulties, may be seen as harmful to a *school's* performance on National Curriculum tests when compared with other schools in the locality, with the consequence that the continuation of mainstream schooling for these children is threatened. From the perspective of those parents whose children are experiencing problems in school, the difficulties involved in gaining access to additional resources, or even to professional help, may create conditions in which professionals are seen as primarily acting in the interests of schools and/or the LEA. Where this is so, parents may feel little confidence in securing their own empowerment through entering into a partnership with professionals.

CONCLUSIONS

This chapter has reviewed the contribution of parents to decision-making in special education assessments. The development of an ideology of 'parents as partners' has been traced to changes in educational philosophy in the post-war period, and the Plowden Report (CACE 1967) has been identified as making a major contribution to the way in which special educational needs were subsequently re-conceptualized by the Warnock Report (DES 1978). It has been argued that different ways of conceptualizing children's 'needs' have important consequences for the role of parents in the decision-making procedures.

Despite the emphasis placed on the contribution of parents to decision-making in special educational assessments by the Warnock Report and the legislation which followed it, parents' experiences continue to be negative. It has been argued that in part this reflects changes in the social and political climate since 1978. As the return to economic down-turn and recession became a portent of wide-ranging global economic change, new political priorities have changed the way in which 'needs' have come to be understood in the education system. The 1980s and 1990s have been characterized by an increasing atomization of needs as they have come, once more, to be represented in terms of individual deficits, failures and personal tragedies. Separated from forms of collective action and decision-making, social disadvantage has been reconstructed as individual despair and responses to that despair have been made dependent upon the outcome of individual negotiation.

The liberal consensus and the professional ethic of service associated with it have been broken and the fragmentation of professional responsibilities which has followed has been an almost inevitable corollary to the atomization of needs. This has given rise to tensions and conflicts in relation to both professional roles and resource allocation. These changes have profound implications for children with special educational needs and for their parents, as the latter increasingly come into conflict with LEAs and their professional advisers. However, it has been further argued that the 'partnership' model contains internal contradictions which negate the possibility of parents being genuinely involved as partners with professionals in decision-making. Pressures on professionals, from a variety of sources, are clearly increasing, but the 'partnership' model treats professional roles as relatively uncomplicated. Professional judgement and action are often characterized (as they are in the Warnock Report) as motivated by disinterested concern with the 'best interests' of their clients, usually assumed to be the child. This may well be an accurate description of how professionals would like to see themselves but it is a view that is becoming increasingly untenable.

Chapter 2

Parents and professionals
The experience of partnership

The 1981 Education Act gave important new rights and entitlements to parents with regard to the procedures for assessing children's special educational needs. These included not only the right to make representations but also the right to participate in decision-making as members of a multi-disciplinary assessment team. Yet, as we saw in Chapter 1, there continues to be strong evidence to suggest that parents remain at a serious disadvantage in their dealings with professionals.

This chapter draws on recent research carried out by the author on the role of parents in special needs assessments to examine their experience of the 1981 Act. It will be argued that there is a clear contradiction between the legal rights given to parents under the 1981 Act and the accounts parents give of the assessment procedures which are supposed to encourage their participation in decision-making. However, it will also be argued that there is evidence to suggest that parents do not passively accept their lack of power and may take action in support of their own objectives during their children's assessments. In doing so parents identify and use sources of power that lie outside the official procedures of the assessment.

INITIATING AN ASSESSMENT

The research literature on parent–professional co-operation is extensive and much of this focuses upon the parents of children identified as having special educational needs. This research has consistently drawn attention to the strains placed on relations between parents and professionals whilst assessments of special needs under the 1981 Education Act are taking place (Goacher *et al.* 1988; Tomlinson 1981; Wood 1988). There may be many reasons for conflict at this stage. It can be an emotionally highly charged time for teachers as well as for parents, and both may experience a sense of frustration with a situation over which they feel themselves to have little control.

Differences between teachers and parents over the decision to initiate an assessment may also reflect wider conflicts of values and perspectives which may have built up over a long period of time. For teachers, the referral of a child for a formal assessment of special educational needs may be motivated by more than a straightforward concern about a child's educational welfare. As one teacher in the study put it: 'The child needs help and so do his teachers.' Similarly, parents' objections to an assessment taking place could reflect their antagonisms towards their children's schools and suspicions about the motivation lying behind a referral: 'They want him out.' On the other hand, these initial objections might be tempered by a perception that professionals from outside the school might get to the bottom of the problem: 'My son needs professional help. The parents can't always do things. We're only guessing. We need someone who knows.' This perhaps explains why parents rarely make any formal objection to assessments being initiated, despite their reservations.

There was no evidence of any attempt on the part of psychologists to misinform parents of their rights in this respect. Indeed psychologists, teachers, doctors and other professionals taking part in the study, perhaps conscious of the presence of a researcher, took pains to inform parents of their rights. However, it was not altogether clear to what extent parents were aware of their option to register opposition to the commencement of statementing procedures. The apparent mismatch between information given to parents by professionals and the perceptions parents had of the information they had been given was a recurring theme. What it is possible to say is that some parents, at least, felt they had no real option but to accept the decision to initiate an assessment.

One mother described what she felt to be a *fait accompli*: 'It was the head teacher who first mentioned it to me. He said that the school psychologist will be seeing John and will want to see me too.' Another parent believed that the decision to assess her child in the final year of his primary schooling had more to do with administrative convenience than with any desire on the part of the LEA to help her child. 'They are going to assess him to see if he's going to big school or to a special school.'

For a significant minority of parents (ten) the decision to start statementing was actually perceived as a welcome relief, particularly where parents' own attempts to get help in the past seemed to have been ignored. Yet the parents of only one child appeared to be entirely happy about the level of involvement they had in the decision to begin the statementing procedures. It might not be insignificant that these parents were, on any of the criteria most commonly accepted, middle class, making this an exceptional case. Their discovery that 'expert' advice on children's behaviour was provided by the LEA's schools' psychological service, and that this could be made available to a child whose education had up to that point been provided by fee-paying schools, was seen by them as a 'godsend': 'It was very traumatic. . . . We'd reached a situation where there was no school, no tutor, and we had to have him at home.'

Once the assessment was under way Gavin's father commented that at the outset

> we had very little knowledge of the system and the procedures of the formal assessment but we were very happy with the way in which the educational professionals in particular stepped in to assist us. It is unfortunate that so many more people are not aware of what is available.

Other parents, although happy about the decision to initiate a formal assessment, were less enthusiastic about the help they had received from professionals in getting the process started. In four cases parents believed that the decision to initiate an assessment had only been taken because of their own perseverance in the face of professional lack of interest or even outright opposition. One mother claimed that: 'Every time I have tried to instigate help for John I have got nowhere.' Another parent catalogued her attempts to get help after 'I'd had so much trouble at school'.

> I rang Pear Tree House School for autistic children, not that I thought he was autistic but we didn't know who to ask and we found out about Pear Tree House from a friend. Pear Tree House told us to ring the Swallowdale Centre – it's a mental handicapped hospital. I spoke to a doctor there who said Peter was too young to be referred to them and suggested that I should contact the children's unit at the hospital. When I did this I got put through to a medical social worker who suggested I should get in touch with the Children's Guidance Service. When I contacted them I spoke to a social worker who suggested I should see an educational psychologist. I said I didn't know there was one. I rang him and he came to see me straight away. He asked me why the school hadn't suggested a child psychologist. The school never suggested anything to do. I was helped by my friend. We racked our brains till we thought of something.

Even when parents were successful in getting to see a psychologist, confusion could remain about whether or not an assessment was taking place. The parents of at least two children in the study believed, following a meeting they had requested with an educational psychologist, that a formal assessment under the 1981 Education Act had been started. In both these cases parents were mistaken in their belief. In one of these cases Mrs Parker had asked her son's head teacher for a meeting with an educational psychologist so that she could set in motion an assessment of his needs. Mrs Parker and John were duly seen by an educational psychologist. Twelve months later the situation in school was deteriorating and Mrs Parker reported her son's head teacher as saying that there were now 'serious problems and statementing should be started'.

> I thought it already had been started when I asked the educational psychologist to see John the last time. I assumed that once you had asked for a psychologist then the assessment would start, *but obviously the school have to ask for an assessment as well.*
>
> (Author's emphasis)

When this assessment was finally completed Mrs Parker told how 'I felt let down by the psychologist because I had asked for help. If help had been given then he wouldn't need this [special school] now.' Differences between professionals and parents in their perceptions of the outcome of a psychologist's initial involvement probably arose because of different perceptions of the purpose of that involvement.

Parents were generally unaware of the subtle difference between assessments carried out at Warnock's stage 3 and those carried out at Warnock's stages 4 and 5. This was made even more confusing by the fact that what teachers understood to be required by Warnock's stages 1–3 bore little resemblance to the Warnock Committee's own description. For instance, although records of children's progress were kept, these were invariably confined to descriptions of particular incidents and general behaviour. There was some evidence that psychologists tended to become involved at an informal level, prior to the initiation of the formal procedures, when parents were active in promoting the assessment. Where teachers' requests for formal assessment were related to perceptions of children's behaviour problems the procedures were much more likely to be initiated after a single interview with parents and child and without any detailed evidence of in-school preliminary assessment. Thus, it appeared to be the case that where a request for formal assessment was not initiated by teachers it was given less priority, or at least dealt with in a very different manner. This is despite the statutory duty placed on LEAs by the 1981 Education Act to initiate assessment procedures in response to a parental request, unless in the judgement of the LEA there is good reason not to do so.

In the few cases where parents successfully initiated assessment procedures under the 1981 Act this happened (1) as a direct consequence of pressure they were able to bring to bear on the LEA (three cases): 'I requested the statementing procedures to be initiated. The education authority only agreed to do this when I removed Stephen from school. Without a statement they would not be able to place him in an alternative school.'

Or (2) this occurred because the request was supported by teachers at the child's school (three cases).

From the perspective of most parents, however, the difficulties they experienced in getting help reflected the priorities of professionals rather than the needs of their children and themselves. As one mother put it: 'We've been telling them about Philip's behaviour, and how his behaviour has gone downhill, since next to the last year in junior school. They only decided to do something when it got too bad for the teachers.'

PARENTS' VIEWS ABOUT THE PURPOSE OF ASSESSMENT

Perceptions of the purpose of the formal assessment procedures varied quite dramatically amongst participants in these assessments. Whereas teachers and psychologists tended to focus upon concerns relating to children's behaviour in school and to a lesser extent at home, parents were more likely to see the assessment as a way of drawing attention to difficulties they and their children were encountering because of actions which had been taken or not taken by their children's teachers and head teachers. This was evident in fourteen of the twenty-nine cases. By contrast, a slightly smaller group of parents (ten cases) believed that the assessment would lead to diagnosis and treatment of the 'illness' or 'disorder' their children were 'suffering' from. There were fairly clear indications of an overlap between these 'treatment' and 'conflict' models in a number of cases, and indeed one or other of the models might predominate at different stages of an assessment. None the less, this broad classification provides a useful framework for analysing the type of strategies employed by parents during an assessment.

Perceptions of causality in relation to the purpose of assessment

On the whole, teachers initiated assessments with a fairly clear idea of the outcome they expected from this action. The purpose might be the removal of a child from their mainstream school (fifteen cases); the re-integration of a child into mainstream school (two cases) or an attempt to gain additional resources (eight cases). The remaining four cases were parental referrals. Teachers' perceptions of the causes of problem behaviour were significant in relation to their decision to seek outside professional assistance and in relation to their expectations of the assessment outcome. In Chapter 7 it will be argued that the identification of 'unmanageable' behaviour as 'disturbed' has major implications for teachers' conceptualizations of their own professional skills.

The opportunity the assessment procedures appeared to provide for identifying the cause of children's problem behaviour was seen by many parents, initially at least, as a very good reason for being co-operative, despite differences they might have with their children's schools over the actual management of that behaviour. In ten cases there was evidence of parents claiming that their child was 'disturbed' or 'abnormal' in some way. 'There's got to be something that causes these problems', claimed one parent in welcoming the assessment of her son. Another mother was typical of this group of parents when she stated that 'I could understand it if it was neglect but it's not. It's got to be something in his head.' For these parents the hope was that the assessment would identify the causes of their children's 'disorders'. Thus one commented: 'I thought the doctor would have found out what was wrong with him [her son]. He's nothing like all the other children in the family. To me there's something not right. It could be a genetic disorder.'

Ford *et al.* (1982) have argued that the enduring popularity of pseudo-medical accounts of children's behaviour in these cases is related to the relief many parents feel on being offered an explanation for the behaviour, which does not imply any moral or social criticism of them as parents. Thus parents may feel absolved from feeling that they have been bad parents and may even join in victimizing their child. The attempt by these parents to negotiate a shared consensus about the purpose of the assessment based upon the child's personality deficits was important if their own needs were to be met by the assessment.

It could be argued that teachers also tended to adopt a medical model of emotional and behavioural difficulties. In sixteen cases teachers identified children's behaviour as 'disturbed', and there was a common view that 'disturbed' behaviour was in some sense qualitatively different from the behaviour of 'normal' children, with children whose behaviour was characterized as 'disruptive' being included in this latter group. As with parents, the identification of deficits within the child served to absolve teachers from responsibility for the child's failure in school. However, in addition to identifying children's behaviour as 'disturbed', teachers in eight cases also emphasized 'disturbed' or 'chaotic' family life as a causal factor responsible for disturbing classroom behaviour.

Despite the emphasis placed on causal accounts of emotional and behavioural difficulties by teachers, these accounts differed from those of the children's parents in an important respect. Implicit in the use by parents of a medical label was the idea that the assessment would result in the discovery of forms of 'treatment'. A psychologist in one case had suggested to parents that their child's reading difficulties might be a cause of his behaviour problems in school. This explanation was seized upon by these parents, and when they were later interviewed by the researcher they commented that

> We'd always assumed that his behaviour problems had been causing the problems with his reading. Today was the first time that anyone had said that there was a definite link between reading and behaviour, but reading as the cause. It's made a big difference finding out this information today. There's been a positive outcome from this session today because they can focus on dealing with it now. It does spell out a lot of hope.

When the psychologist was interviewed by the researcher he acknowledged that reading difficulties might be a factor with some bearing upon Nick's problems in school but, none the less, maintained that it was unlikely that these would be the major cause of his disruptive behaviour in school. An unstable home environment was seen by the psychologist as the most significant factor responsible for Nick's behaviour in school.

Differences in the precise meanings attached to the model of needs adopted by parents and teachers were related to their different perceptions of their own needs. For teachers, the significance of the label 'disturbed' lay more in the personal (reduction of stress), professional (reskilling) and financial (resources) outcomes that would be expected to follow once consensus had been reached about the validity of the label in a particular case. Both parents and teachers used the label to shift responsibility for children's difficulties away from themselves, and usually on to the child. Thus teachers and parents could have a mutual interest in developing a shared consensus about the significance of causal factors 'responsible' for the child's behaviour. However, the notion of 'treatment' often implicit in parental expectations of the assessment reflected a continuing commitment towards their children. Even when children were eventually placed in residential education (and in three cases in the care of the local authority), the parents in this study retained some level of responsibility for the care of their children. For teachers the situation was very different.

Once a decision had been taken to remove a child from mainstream school the responsibilities of teachers in that school towards the child were at an end. The identification of a child's special educational needs legitimized the cessation of that responsibility.

Home–school conflict and the assessment of special educational needs

In twenty-four of the twenty-nine cases considered in this study conflict between home and school was a common feature. This conflict between home and school could reflect the presence of very different values operating within each. For one mother this clash of values was summed up as follows: 'The rule of the school is that if anyone hits them they haven't to hit back. They've got to see a teacher. Our rule has always been if anyone hits you, you hit them back.'

The reports compiled by teachers for the LEA's assessment identified home circumstances as causal or contributory factors in only eight cases. At first sight this latter finding appears to be inconsistent with evidence from research by Moses and Croll (1987), who found that the cause of learning and behaviour difficulties most commonly reported by teachers was home circumstances. However, interviews with teachers suggested a discrepancy between their personal accounts of the reasons for children's difficulties and their formal reporting of these (reports which would be read by parents). In the former, much greater emphasis was placed on what were considered to be inadequate home environments. The reluctance of teachers to make negative references to children's home circumstances in their formal reports probably reflected a desire to avoid open conflict with parents.

In only one case did a teacher refer to factors within the school as contributing to a child's difficulties, and even here there was no reference to these problems in the school's written report. This case was exceptional in that there was evidence of a widespread demoralization amongst the staff at the school linked to serious under-funding and under-staffing over a lengthy period of time. Teachers at this school accepted that these circumstances had made it difficult to manage children whose behaviour was difficult. Despite these circumstances the head teacher justified his decision to refer a child on the grounds that the child's behaviour was aggravating what was already a difficult situation, disregarding the possibility that it might be those circumstances which were responsible for the child's behaviour.

In three further cases teachers did express forceful criticism of the work of their colleagues in schools which children in the sample had previously attended. Once again, however, there was generally no mention of these criticisms in teachers' written reports, although they might be interpreted as containing 'coded' messages intended for LEA officers but not parents. Nick's new head teacher, for instance, wrote that 'up to this point [that is, in his old school] Nick's mother has only been involved in school with his behaviour. Achievement has never been used as a motivator but this could be a very important step as a condition for successful work with Nick.'

Differences between parents and teachers during special educational needs assessments have been well documented (Dyson 1987; Moses and Croll 1987; Wood 1988). However, interviews with many parents participating in this research revealed a surprising depth of anger, distrust and contempt for the schools attended by their children. Many complaints were recited ranging from minor but repetitive instances of victimization to quite serious allegations of physical and mental abuse. There was a strong feeling held by virtually all these parents that they had been made the scapegoats for the failings of teachers. Moreover, the power held by teachers could make the assessment an uncomfortable experience for parents. 'She seemed to be assessing me rather than Stephen. It's like she's shifting the blame on to me.'

None the less, parents were not slow in making their feelings known to psychologists. Thus one parent, speaking of her son, argued that

> I don't get him effing and blinding on the street like they're suggesting he does at school. They must create the problem at school. If a child's a cheeky child they're going to be cheeky all the time, not just at school. So they must create the problem themselves.

In only one case in the study was there any evidence of action being taken as a direct result of parents' complaints about the treatment of a child in school. In this case the parent was supported by the psychologist *and by the school's head teacher* who used the assessment to change practices within a particular classroom. Apart from this case there was no evidence that complaints made by parents lead to the scope of an assessment being extended to cover the curriculum or school/classroom management.

There were many complaints made by parents about alleged double standards within schools. A graphic example of this was provided by one parent who compared the way a secondary school had treated her son when he was being assessed with what happened to her daughter in the same school:

What has happened with David has made things worse for his sister. Collette was hit by a teacher in front of other children. When I complained I was told it wouldn't happen again. The teacher wasn't suspended but David was for hitting someone in the playground.

One could go on for a very long time reporting parents' accounts of incidents like this, but without corroboration it would be pointless to do so. Within the constraints of the methodology employed in this research it would be impossible to make any judgement about the validity of these complaints and allegations. What they do illustrate is the chasm that very often exists between parents and schools by the time formal assessment has been started. As one parent succinctly put it: 'I hate the school. I really hate that school.' In consequence, by the time the formal assessment procedures were initiated the relationship between parents and school had so seriously broken down that any possibility of 'partnership' between these two participants in the assessment was out of the question.

PARTNERSHIP AND PROFESSIONAL ROLES

Information to parents

The 1981 Education Act gave parents a right of access to all information used by the LEA in making its decision about provision for children identified as having special educational needs. To this end the Act requires LEAs to make available to parents all the reports prepared by professionals contributing advice for the statement. There was no evidence of LEAs failing to meet their obligations under the Act in this respect. Despite this, the most common complaint voiced by parents was that they lacked adequate information, and that this impeded their ability to contribute effectively to the decision-making process. This complaint not only related to the final decision taken on completion of the assessment but also to key stages along the way. The LEA's intentions were often unclear to parents – 'I don't know whether the assessment was because of his behaviour or because of his learning problems at school' – as were the stages that it would pass through – 'I don't know what the assessment will involve or who will contribute to it.'

Few parents appeared to have any understanding of what their rights within the procedures were. According to one mother, after being told her son's special educational needs were to be assessed: 'The educational psychologist said he'd have to go for a medical. That was it really. All we saw was her [the educational psychologist] and went for a medical. There was no explanation of our rights.' For some parents the absence of information from the LEA was seen as having sinister overtones. 'There was a total lack of communication – not telling me any results. I felt more threatened than informed by the assessment.'

The accounts given by parents of how they had been deprived of information contrasted sharply with the accounts given by professionals of the information they had given to parents. The methodology of the research was useful in this respect because it provided evidence in support of the psychologists' claims. Although there was evidence in two cases to suggest that parents had been deliberately misinformed about the assessment of their children, in the remaining cases observations of professionals' interviews with parents revealed that the former had provided parents with fairly comprehensive and objective descriptions of the procedures of the assessment. In addition, advice had been offered about who should be contacted if further information was required. This evidence suggests that the parents in this study were under a misapprehension when they claimed they had been given very little or no information. Yet, as will be argued in Chapter 3, the exchange of information between professionals and parents involves far more complex issues than might first appear to be the case.

What was striking from the cases looked at in this study was the apparent lack of detailed and accessible written information for parents. The schools provided no written information of their own to guide parents through the procedures of the assessment. The LEAs, by contrast, did have written guidance for parents but in only one LEA was there any evidence of this being consistently made available to parents. In this LEA a leaflet explaining the stages of the assessment was given to parents by an educational social worker who had specific responsibilities within the authority for liaison with parents of children with special educational needs. This leaflet was generally well received by parents, though one mother did describe it as 'too simple'. Parents in this LEA, however, believed the educational social worker himself to be the most useful source of information because of the regular contact between them. In the two other participating LEAs there was no evidence of the available literature actually going out to parents.

One educational psychologist had written a short booklet on the assessment procedures which she gave to parents on the occasion of her first meeting with them. This was quite detailed and might well have been useful to some parents, although in one case the booklet was actually a source of the parents' subsequent misunderstanding. After reading through the booklet which the psychologist had left with her, Katy's mother explained to the researcher how this had helped her to understand why Katy's school had been so concerned about her behaviour. 'She could be dyslexic because that's what this booklet says. That's where only half the brain works. We've got a better understanding of her now we've read about this dyslexia.' In fact, although the psychologist believed Katy to have learning difficulties she did not consider that these were related to 'dyslexia'.

It is clearly impossible to take into account every possible interpretation that parents might place on information they are given during the course of an assessment. Parents have an interest in promoting a particular view of their child's needs. In pursuing this, information from the assessment may be used, however tenuously the link, to legitimize their own views. Moreover, the assessment process can be a very stressful one for parents, and the high level of anxiety that parents frequently experience during their child's assessment does not help when they are trying to make a balanced judgement about their child's educational needs.

It does appear to be clear from the evidence obtained in this study that LEAs and their professional advisers still have a long way to go in promoting effective communications with parents. It would be wrong to generalize from these findings to the quality of communications with parents in other LEAs but there is growing evidence that the picture is not dissimilar in other authorities (Goacher *et al.* 1988). Even where, as was the case in one of the LEAs in the study, serious attempts are made to provide parents with ready access to information at all stages, these procedures, welcomed as they were by parents, did not stop their complaints about a lack of information. This perhaps suggests that problems relating to the nature and exchange of information actually involve difficulties that cannot be resolved simply by improving the flow of information to parents.

Parents' perceptions of professional roles

During the course of an assessment of a child's special educational needs his or her parents will come into contact with a great many professionals, including teachers, a doctor and a psychologist. These professionals, along with the parents themselves, constitute the core members of the multidisciplinary team charged under the 1981 Education Act with providing the LEA with advice on the nature of a child's needs. Yet the relative weakness of parents as members of this 'team' is underlined by the confusion they frequently experience with regard to the contribution of each of these professionals to the overall assessment. This confusion is one that may be shared by professional participants in the assessment also.

Clinical medical officers, for instance, have a somewhat ambiguous role in the assessment of children with emotional and behavioural difficulties and they frequently see their own contribution as peripheral, confined to medical screening. Parents may also be confused about the role of the clinical medical officer. The parents of five of the twenty-nine children in the study understood the medical assessment as a screening procedure which might lead to some physical cause of their children's difficulties being revealed 'just in case anything medical was causing his problems – something inside him that we've never noticed before'. However, the remaining parents expressed their ignorance of the purpose of the medical examination. When these parents were asked why their children had been medically examined their replies were in a similar vein. 'I've not got a clue. He was there for an hour and a half but I haven't got a clue. I didn't get any comments about what they thought.'

Although in some cases parents saw doctors as a possible source of 'some fairly useful information', generally the contribution of the clinical medical officer to the assessment was seen by parents as an irrelevance. 'I still don't know why he had it. I think it's a legal thing. It could be he was a slow learner [but] I can't see the relevance of sounding his chest and looking down his ears.' Irrelevant as it might be, the medical examination could be a source of parental anxiety. 'It was almost like they were looking for abuse or something. We didn't know why he was going for a medical.'

If the contribution of the clinical medical officer was sometimes seen as an irrelevance, the contribution of the psychologist was seen as anything but. However, parents' accounts of the role and contribution of the psychologist to the assessment varied widely. For the parents of two children in this study the psychological assessment was perceived to be concerned with finding out the ability level of their children, 'whether he's doing the things he should be doing'. A larger number of parents saw the psychologist as someone 'who finds out about children's problems'. In ten cases this was related to physiological deficits or to the psychological 'disorders' parents believed their children to be suffering from. According to these parents the psychologist's contribution to the assessment of a child was more likely to involve 'testing how his brain pattern works'.

The fact that psychologists did not always share this view of their role was sometimes a source of consternation to parents. One father, for instance, questioned whether his child's psychologist was qualified to carry out the sort of assessment that was needed: 'I don't know how he can find out what's wrong with Bryan when he's not medically qualified.' Other parents were also less than enthusiastic about the psychologist's involvement. For one mother, who claimed to have been desperately seeking help over a long period of time, the decision to carry out a psychological assessment was greeted with a degree of cynicism: 'If anything's wrong at school they get a child psychologist but if you ask for a child psychologist they do nothing.'

It is difficult to quantify the level of parental satisfaction with the services provided by psychologists. There were parents in the study who clearly were happy with the contribution made by psychologists to the assessment even though they might not be happy with the outcome of the assessment as a whole. On the other hand, when parents were unhappy with aspects of the assessment it was not always clear whether the source of this dissatisfaction lay in their perceptions of how they had been treated by psychologists or whether an unsatisfactory outcome had coloured their view of the psychologist's role. There was, however, clear evidence of a drop in the level of parental satisfaction with psychologists as assessments progressed towards their conclusion. Once the assessment had been completed many parents felt bewildered and let down:

> I thought that when everything was all over I would get to see Dr Brown [the psychologist] and he would explain everything to me but I never saw him again. I thought he would come and see me and go over the last twelve months. I was always there when the teachers sent for me so I thought it would have been his job to see me. All I got was their reports with things written on that I didn't know what they meant. Surely as a parent you should have the right to be told what it all means. After twelve months he could have done something. If I'd been seeing a child for twelve months I think I would have wrote a statement and sent it to the parent to say what I'd done. I don't know what he's getting paid for. He told me at the beginning that they didn't do anything behind your back but I've never even had a letter off him. If I go out of my way and let them do all this and go to these meetings I could have got a response from them.

This view of psychologists was almost universal amongst the parents in the study by the time the assessments had been completed.

Psychologists' written reports were a particular source of annoyance to parents. There was a strong feeling expressed that these were 'incomprehensible'. 'Some of the things they wrote I don't understand what they mean – test results – Burt re-arranged reading scores.' Another parent, when interviewed by the researcher, read out an extract from the psychologist's report: "'Neale Analysis of Reading Ability, Form A. CA = 12.11, RA Accuracy = 9.11, RA Comprehension = 9.5. RA Rate = 13.0+." How am I supposed to know what RA means?'

A possible explanation for the form taken by psychologist's reports, and one frequently put forward by psychologists themselves, is that the report serves a dual purpose. On the one hand, the report is a source of information for parents but, on the other hand, it is also written with the aim of making out a case to the LEA for the provision of additional resources. It might not be unreasonable to suggest that the technical nature of these reports could also serve the function of legitimating the central role of the psychologist in the assessment procedures on the grounds of the psychologist's technical knowledge and skills.

Partnership and decision-making

Parents commonly believe that they have been excluded from decision-making by professionals during special needs assessments. This view contrasts sharply with how professionals themselves see the role of parents in the decision-making process. The latter frequently express beliefs about the way in which children's home circumstances significantly contribute to the difficulties experienced by these children in school. It does not follow from this, however, that professionals are unsympathetic to these families. Interviews with psychologists, in particular, revealed a concern that parents should be encouraged to participate in decision-making and that they should not be unfairly persuaded or manipulated into making decisions about which they are unhappy. None the less, psychologists felt they had an important role as professional advisers to parents and that it was therefore both legitimate and appropriate to offer guidance which would influence their decision-making. This, of course, assumes that the role of the psychologist as parental adviser or advocate is unproblematic. This is far from so.

Observations of psychologists' interviews with parents did provide evidence to support the claims made by the former that they were anxious for parents to be partners in decision-making. In these circumstances it was surprising to find that parents not only felt that they lacked the power to affect the outcome of their children's assessments but also that they believed they had been intentionally disempowered by the actions of professionals. For some parents the only access they believed themselves to have to the decision-making process was through their own direct action in confronting and challenging the actions of professionals.

> The only time I can remember being included in anything was when I went to a meeting at the education offices with the welfare officer, the psychologist and the welfare officer's supervisor. I wasn't even invited. My mum told me to go and say I wanted to be there.

Yet the psychologist in this case had regularly met with this parent to keep her informed of the progress of her son's assessment, to consult with her and to discuss different options for the future. At one point during the assessment, after her boy had been permanently excluded from his school, the psychologist bowed to this mother's wishes and against his own judgement persuaded the LEA to provide an alternative mainstream placement so that he could be given another chance. One conclusion that could be drawn from this is that the sense of powerlessness felt by parents may in part represent an attempt to rationalize decisions they have found difficult to take. In other words, beliefs about powerlessness may reflect a desire to shift responsibility for those decisions on to the shoulders of professionals. This was certainly the view of at least one psychologist who took part in the study. In discussing the case of a child in the sample this psychologist argued that despite a lengthy period of parental opposition to a residential placement their eventual agreement with this outcome reflected the 'fact' that 'This was what they really wanted all the way along'. If these parents had been successful in opposing this placement they would have been forced to retain responsibility for the 'problem'.

It is impossible to test the veracity of such a conclusion. The logic of this argument was explicitly rejected by the parents themselves. It could equally be argued that the parents had been offered a 'forced' choice, the crucial missing element in the decision-making equation being an option that would have allowed them to reject the residential placement for their child whilst providing family as well as school support. Thus, it could be argued that the real consequence of parents being presented with 'forced' choices is the legitimation of professionals' power over parents. This was certainly the view of one parent, who argued that

> I was given my chance to have a say but no-one told me what my rights were or what I could do. . . . In other words I had no choice. He had to go to a [day] special school because he had been accepted there. The only alternative was a boarding school.

In another case the researcher observed that a psychologist had taken great care to consult with parents about the details of their child's assessment. This extended to allowing them the right to correct factual inaccuracies in his report and add riders with regard to any matter where their own judgement differed from that of the psychologist. Despite this fairly extraordinary level of consultation, on the assessment being concluded these parents complained that 'The educational psychologist gave us the right to make any alterations to his report we wished but we couldn't change the recommendation about residential school.'

Speculation regarding the truth of claims made by parents and by psychologists is perhaps a pointless exercise. It is unlikely in any case that any one of these perspectives represents the truth in some absolute sense. What is important to note, however, are the very significant differences that are evident between the way professionals and parents perceive their 'common experience', even where there is evidence of professionals supporting parents' wishes despite their own reservations. This suggests that the difficulties and conflicts parents experience during their children's assessments do not necessarily have their origins in an opposition of interests between professionals and parents, although the wider social context within which assessment is located does have implications for the ability of parents and professionals to enter into effective partnerships.

STEPPING OUTSIDE THE ACT

At face value the 1981 Education Act establishes a co-operative framework. In practice, however, the bureaucratization of the multi-disciplinary assessment procedures may lead to a situation in which the main outcome of parental involvement in an assessment is the legitimation of decisions taken by professionals. Many parents believe that their own contribution to that assessment is only taken seriously when they support what is said by professionals. Moreover, a sharp contrast can be detected between the view of professionals that assessments involve a high degree of consensus and the view expressed by parents that their agreement with decisions taken by professionals stems from a belief that no other choice is possible or realistic. Often this breakdown of communication is never apparent to professionals, which may lead parents to adopt strategies aimed at achieving their own objectives independently of the official procedures.

In one case the mother of a 14-year-old boy, Stephen, felt her local education authority was acting unjustly in denying her requests for her son to be assessed under the 1981 Education Act. This refusal to initiate the assessment was made even though six months previously Stephen had been permanently excluded from his mainstream high school and yet no alternative school placement had been offered. From his mother's perspective the fact that no mainstream school in the district would accept Stephen on to its roll in itself meant that he had a special educational need.

However, she also argued that another event that had taken place shortly before Stephen's exclusion from school indicated the suitability of a residential school placement in his case (Stephen had been the victim of a sexual assault by an older boy in the neighbourhood which, it was alleged, had led to his experiencing severe adjustment difficulties in the home and community).

Local authority officers were not unsympathetic to the difficulties Stephen was experiencing but they felt the problem was being exaggerated by his mother and that the difficulty in finding an alternative mainstream school placement had actually been caused by her insistence that Stephen should be admitted to a residential school. Given the resource implications of a residential school placement and the financial constraints under which the officers saw the authority to be operating they had delayed any decision about initiating statementing procedures. They reported to Mrs Blackledge that there were no available places in the residential school normally used by this LEA and that statementing could not be initiated until after the completion of informal pre-assessment procedures, which would include a report drawn up by an educational psychologist. Yet the delay in beginning the assessment occurred despite the fact that a confidential report from the educational psychologist already existed. This report recommended the commencement of statementing and an emergency placement in a residential setting pending the completion of a full assessment.

Despite the LEA's delaying strategy, Mrs Blackledge did finally obtain the agreement of the local authority to initiate the statementing procedures and place Stephen in residential education. She did this by obtaining information about the LEA's policy with regard to special school placements (though this did not involve specific information about Stephen's case) from a friend who worked at the school Mrs Blackledge wanted her son to attend and then persuading her local MP to take up her case. The authority alleged that Mrs Blackledge's friend had acted unprofessionally but, regardless of these protestations, within 24 hours of the MP's intervention an emergency placement had been found for Stephen in the residential school and the statementing procedures initiated.

A second case illustrates the conflict that can arise between parents and professionals when each has a different perception of the purpose of a formal assessment. Where such conflict occurs the relationship between information and control may lead to parental disempowerment, but it may also force parents into taking actions which bypass and neutralize the operation of the official procedures. At the outset, these parents believed that close co-operation with the professionals involved in the assessment of their son would give them the power to effect improvements in the quality of education that he was receiving. Towards the latter stages the assessment procedures were seen by the parents as effectively removing their ability to contribute meaningfully to the decision-making process.

For twelve months Tom, who at the time the research was conducted was 9 years old, had been attending an off-site unit for disruptive children on two and a half days each week. This placement followed the break-up of his parents' marriage which was acknowledged by his mother, but not his father, as having a serious effect upon Tom's behaviour. After the break-up the parents were awarded joint custody and Tom resided for part of the week with each. Mrs Jones felt that this arrangement was itself disruptive and should be changed. Mr Jones did not agree. He felt that Tom caused him no problems and it was Tom's relationship with his mother that was at the root of the behaviour problem.

Tom had recently been referred by his mainstream school to the Psychological Service for assessment under the 1981 Act because his teachers felt they should receive additional support for Tom's periods in mainstream school. The educational psychologist in this case felt that even more drastic measures might be required. In his view Tom was being used as a pawn in the relationship between his parents and unless his parents came to an arrangement whereby 'a more stable home situation' was provided, Tom would benefit from a residential school placement.

Tom's mother was highly critical of the way the mainstream school was handling him but agreed to the assessment believing that it might result in some additional support for Tom in his mainstream classroom. She also hoped that an assessment would lead to a better understanding of Tom's problems in school. Once the assessment had begun Mrs Jones soon became disillusioned. She complained bitterly about the lack of information she was receiving. This, perhaps, reflected a lack of clarity about the purpose of the assessment and the conflicting expectations she and Tom's teachers had of its outcome. Mrs Jones expected feedback and dialogue focusing upon the development of an intervention strategy. When Mrs Jones later challenged the educational psychologist she was told she should have contacted the educational social worker designated by the LEA as the 'named person'. Mrs Jones couldn't recollect having been informed of this. None the less, having her role in the assessment limited to receiving information back from an educational social worker was not what she had expected. 'We didn't ask for it [the assessment] . . . it was the education system who said it should be done, they invited themselves in . . . if I accept them into my home I don't expect them to disappear for twelve months!' The slow progress of the assessment and the limited information she had received were seen by Mrs Jones as creating new problems rather than resolving existing ones: 'It introduces so much trauma . . . you're getting all the criticism all the time but you're not getting any information because it takes so long.'

Access to information was not the only problem Mrs Jones faced. A lack of common agreement over the objectives of the assessment was something she had not anticipated. Whereas she believed the assessment would be concerned with addressing the needs of the whole family, establishing an objective base line from which she and her ex-husband could identify how their differences were affecting Tom, the educational psychologist refused to become involved in this area arguing that 'It's difficult if I'm to remain neutral.' Yet the educational psychologist was willing to use this dispute to justify his recommendation of residential schooling.

Mrs Jones was dissatisfied that little attention appeared to have been given to Tom's problems in school. She had been told on one occasion by the educational psychologist that Tom's behaviour problems might have been the result of frustration over reading difficulties. She had found this information to be very positive 'because they can focus on dealing with it now, it spells out a lot of hope'. Yet she felt that little had been done to address this problem in school and that if she now accepted residential school she would be giving up on Tom. None the less, the psychologist's recommendation continued to be residential schooling. Mrs Jones's response was, 'No way am I going to agree with that.' On the other hand, on a different occasion she expressed feelings of depression and powerlessness in the face of the professional advice she had received, conceding that she might allow Tom to go to residential school if it could be shown that it was in his best interests.

Once the psychologist had recommended residential schooling in his report Mrs Jones expressed little confidence in her 'rights' under the law. What was more important to her was that she should play an equal part in defining the nature of her child's needs. Whilst at the initial stage of the assessment the process had been seen by her as an opportunity for enhancing her role in the decision-making process it was now seen as restricting her decision-making power. Her perception of powerlessness within the framework of the Act was ultimately the basis for Mrs Jones's decision to abandon reliance upon those procedures. She moved house and, with the co-operation of the head teacher of a nearby school, changed Tom's mainstream school and withdrew him from the off-site unit. The educational psychologist and LEA were now presented with a *fait accompli.* According to Mrs Jones they had little option in the circum-stances but to allow her decision a 'chance to fail'.

DISEMPOWERMENT BY PARTNERSHIP?

The 1981 Education Act clearly states the procedures that must be fol-lowed to ensure parental involvement in the decision-making process. It identifies the range of information that must be made available to parents and establishes their right to submit evidence and advice to the LEA. Procedures are also set out under which parents can seek clarification, state objections and appeal against recommendations. The 1993 Education Act has restated these procedures as well as providing parents with some additional rights, notably a reformed and more powerful appeals tribunal. A strong case can be put forward, therefore, to demonstrate that decisions cannot be taken without full consultation with parents and due deference being given to their views.

In practice there is considerable evidence that parents do not feel empowered by the rights they have been given under the 1981 Act. Although at this stage it is difficult to evaluate the likely impact of changes brought in by the 1993 Education Act and the DFE's Code of Practice, it has been argued in this chapter that the difficulties experienced by parents do not primarily arise because they are excluded from participation in the official procedures, but rather because they lack the power which would make it possible to use their rights effectively. This distinction between 'rights' and 'power' is an important one and yet it is one that is frequently disregarded. Thus, the concepts of 'disclosure' and 'partnership' may themselves operate as disempowering forces as the multi-disciplinary process is used by LEAs to maintain their control over the allocation of resources. In these circumstances parents are marginalized not because professionals deliberately exclude them but because their lack of control over the availability and allocation of resources means that they are denied the opportunity to influence how 'needs' are conceptualized – whether they are to be understood solely by reference to the child or whether they are understood in terms of the interrelationship between participants in the assessment and the relationship between different social contexts to which that assessment is itself related. In this respect parents have much in common with those other members of the multi-disciplinary team, par-ticularly clinical medical officers, who also have no control over LEA resources and who therefore lack the power to negotiate on equal terms with teachers and psychologists. The resignation of parents to the inevi-tability of outcomes which in their eyes are unsatisfactory may be the consequence of their recognition that they are powerless to contribute to the conceptual framework within which their children's needs are assessed.

Mrs Jones and Mrs Blackledge were exceptions because they refused to accept the proposals put forward by their professional advisers. Whereas at first they had welcomed their children's assessments, later they came to believe that they had no say in the objectives that had been set by those assessments. Denied, in their eyes, the opportunity to make genuine contributions to decisions being taken by professionals about their children's needs, they challenged those decisions in the only way they now believed was possible. That is, they rejected their roles as partners in the multi-disciplinary process and challenged the authority of the professionals by stepping outside the framework imposed by the Act. In doing so they successfully forced their LEAs to acknowledge alternative conceptualizations of their children's needs, conceptualizations which carried with them quite different implications for the outcome of the formal assessment process from those envisaged by other participants in the LEA's formal assessment. Yet, to achieve these objectives from the assessment Mrs Jones and Mrs Blackledge found it necessary to identify and pursue sources of strength outside the formal procedures.

CONCLUSION

This chapter has examined parents' experiences of the 1981 Education Act procedures for assessing children's special educational needs. These have been contrasted with accounts of these same procedures given by professionals. The decision to initiate an assessment has been considered, along with conflicting perceptions of the purpose of the assessment, parents' perceptions of the roles of professionals in the assessment and the relevance of the notion of 'partnership' to the decision-making process. It has been argued that there is little evidence of multi-disciplinary collaboration in the assessment of children with special educational needs. This is despite the emphasis the 1981 Education Act places on identifying the needs of the whole child. Research evidence reviewed in this chapter suggests that in practice multi-disciplinary co-operation tends to be restricted to the completion of bureaucratic procedures rather than any genuine attempt at what Goacher *et al.* (1988) refer to as 'collective assessment'. In these circumstances, parents may most effectively empower themselves within the official procedures by the actions they take outside those channels.

Chapter 3

Barriers to partnership

When one talks to teachers, psychologists and other professionals working with children whose special educational needs are being assessed, the high level of commitment these professionals have to parental involvement soon becomes clear. In my own experience, almost without exception professionals who work with children believe that the fullest possible involvement of parents in the assessment and decision-making procedures is a necessary condition of those procedures operating in the best interests of the child. This is not to say that professionals are unaware of the possibility of conflicts of interest between children and their parents; nor are they blind to the ways in which both children and their parents can try to manipulate the assessment procedures for their own ends. Indeed, part of the difficulty professionals experience in these cases – and, it has to be said, part of the enormous skill and compassionate understanding which they exercise in their professional judgements – arises from dealing with a wide range of competing interests and needs. Rarely do professionals believe themselves to have god-like powers to ride roughshod over the concerns, anxieties and fallibilities of parents, even where parenting skills leave a great deal to be desired. Child-care professionals know better than anybody that conflicts of interest and need between children and their parents are never unambiguous. Maintaining the integrity of that relationship wherever this is at all possible is an important professional goal and one that commands widespread commitment from professionals. It is also consistent with the ethical codes of their professional organizations (see, for example, Association of Educational Psychologists 1992) and with the recommendations of the Warnock Report (DES 1978), the statutory requirements of the 1981 Education Act, and the advice of the DES (1983, 1989a) and DFE (1994).

It will always be possible to find a small number of cases where there is evidence of parents being deliberately denied access to information, and clearly issues are raised about the quality of professional practice in those cases. Whilst it is important to identify and eliminate 'bad practice', to focus upon these instances alone would lead to an oversimplified analysis of parent–professional relationships. Unfortunately a characteristic of some of the critical writing on parent–professional relationships has been this moralistic condemnation of professional activity often linked to a stereotypical representation of professional 'social roles'. More interesting, and more important, is an examination of the factors which limit and inhibit the contribution of parents to an assessment, disempowering them in the decision-making process even when professionals are actively committed to facilitating parent–professional partnership. Such an analysis not only helps to develop an understanding of parent–professional relationships but also helps to explore the multi-dimensional role of professionals in child-care settings.

This chapter begins by looking at the culture of the assessment process and how communication between professionals and parents may be affected by the nature of that culture. It goes on to examine how professional interaction within that culture may inhibit open communication with parents and how, in consequence, parents may be perceived as 'problems'. Finally in this chapter, the significance and role of the professional interview with parents is considered. It is argued that the interaction within these interviews is itself a key part of the decision-making process involving the negotiation of shared perspectives between parents and professionals. The process of negotiation, together with the meanings attached by parents and professionals to shared perspectives, is considered by reference to case-study data from research on the assessment process.

COMMUNICATION AND CULTURE

In twenty-six of the twenty-nine cases followed through in this research parents insisted at one stage or another that they had been given no information about the assessment, or key aspects of it, and that they had not been told about their rights in the decision-making process. Simon's mother was typical of many:

> The only information I have about statementing is just because I have a brother-in-law in Glasgow who happens to be a head teacher. He sent me a leaflet. At the moment I feel I'm the last one who's going to know but I feel as Simon's mum I should be the top of the list.

The familiarity professionals have with the 1981 Act and its operation within their LEA may sometimes lead them to make false assumptions about parents' understanding of these procedures. In one case a parent asked for her son to be seen by a psychologist because of the trouble he was continually getting into at infant school. This happened, but twelve months later she was summoned to the school by the head teacher who advised her that there were 'serious problems and statementing should be started'. Mrs Walters felt confused by this:

I thought it had already been started when I asked the educational psychologist to see John last time. I assumed that once you had asked for a psychologist then the assessment would start, but obviously the school have to ask for an assessment as well.

Yet there were also cases where the researcher had been present when detailed information about the assessment procedures had been given to parents. On later occasions parents insisted in interview with the researcher that they had not been given specific pieces of information, only to discover, when discussing particular documents, that the information referred to was contained in one of them.

In one interview both parents were adamant that they had never been told about the 'named person': 'We've never been told about what that is. We've never been told the chain of command.' However, later in the interview these parents produced the original letter from the LEA informing them of the LEA's proposal to initiate a formal assessment. This clearly indicated who the 'named person' was, what his role was and how he was to be contacted. At the time of receiving this information it made little impression on Nick's parents. They had agreed to the assessment on the basis of an agenda of their own: 'I feel that Nick has a reputation but because it's going through a professional series of events, they will look hard at it and consider whether they're singling him out unfairly.' Yet when it became apparent to them that the psychologist was going to recommend Nick's placement in a residential school their perspective on the assessment changed, giving rise to a new need for information and independent advice. It also led them to reconstruct their relationship with the professionals and the LEA. In the context of this reconstructed relationship information that once had not been important now became so. This can be seen, for instance, in the following exchange between Nick's parents and the educational psychologist over the role of the 'named person'. The exchange followed the psychologist's recommendation of a residential school for Nick, which was opposed by his parents.

Mr Morris: What was the educational welfare officer's role in all this?

Psych.:	He's not involved in the assessment. He's the 'named person'. He's a sort of neutral person who will answer any questions.
Mr Morris:	We expected him to be involved in some way. Perhaps he was our link with the system. We would have thought he would have made contact with us.
Mrs Morris:	Why hasn't he?
Psych.:	Pressure of work probably.
Mrs Morris:	But isn't this an important case? You either provide a system or you don't. You can't sit back and say you're too busy.
Mr Morris:	We didn't ask for it. It was the education system who said it should be done. If they say it should be done it's no good coming back and saying our Education Welfare Officer is too busy to see you.

These parents certainly felt they had a legitimate complaint against the LEA. Yet from the LEA's perspective the parents had been told of their rights, and it was up to them to exercise those rights if they felt they needed information or advice. LEAs may, justifiably, be criticized for the ways in which they communicate vital information to parents but this does not imply any deliberate intent on the part of LEAs to withhold information or misinform parents. The assumptions they make about parents in communicating information to them, however, may be entirely inappropriate. In the majority of cases where these misunderstandings occurred parents had accepted that the psychologist's role was to resolve the difficulties their child was having in school and, at the beginning of the assessment procedures at least, these parents expressed confidence in their professional advisers. At this stage bureaucratic messages about the procedures were seen as being of little importance. The real issue for parents was that of what help was to be given their children to resolve the difficulties being encountered. At a later stage when they started to worry about the outcome of the assessment they felt uninformed and unsupported. This was particularly so where they no longer had confidence in the professional advice they were receiving.

At face value the assessment procedures are governed by a set of legal rules which acknowledge the expertise of parents and guarantee their right to participate in decision-making about their children's special educational needs in partnership with professionals. Both the law and 'good practice' dictate that parents are made aware of these rules at the commencement of an assessment. It is in terms of these rules that parents are expected (and allowed) to make sense of the assessment process. The extent to which this is possible is in part dependent upon the willingness of the LEA to communicate information to parents effectively. However, these rules comprise only a part, and often a very small part, of parents' social experience of assessments under the 1981 Education Act.

In addition to the formal rules, the assessment process takes place within a cultural context which is essentially a professional culture to which parents have only limited access. The assessment culture, like all cultures, is built up over time through the interaction taking place within a community of participants. This culture provides a context of meaning within which the formal rules are understood and applied. It is a professional culture, if only because it is professionals who are consistently involved in its development and elaboration. Parents come and go; they are involved in the negotiation of meanings within the culture, but with each new assessment new parents enter the process of negotiation. Lacking the cultural memory that might give them some access to power many parents remain ignorant of significant aspects of the context within which negotiations take place.

PARENTS AS PROBLEMS

Professionals may experience particular difficulty in working in partnership with parents where the professional identifies a conflict of interest between child and parents, as, for instance, where the home situation is seen as the single most important factor responsible for the child's behaviour difficulties. Rather than being seen as partners, parents may be seen as part of the problem (Moses and Croll 1987; Wood 1988) and this may serve to legitimize their disempowerment. Yet the way professionals perceive parents may affect the response of parents to professional intervention. Subsequently, this response may be seen by the professional as further evidence in support of their initial perceptions of inadequate parenting.

Ian, a 7-year-old infant school pupil, was referred by his teachers for formal assessment of his special educational needs following their concern over reports that he might be the victim of physical and sexual abuse. The evidence in support of these allegations was vague and later rejected by a social services investigation that ran parallel to the educational assessment. Ian had recently transferred to this school, and it was acknowledged by his new teachers and an educational psychologist that, whilst he was an exceptionally intelligent boy, his previous school had failed to provide a sufficiently stimulating curriculum for him. Behaviour problems had been present in that school but, despite the efforts of his mother to have him 'seen by someone', no action had been taken until similar problems had surfaced in his new school.

In drawing her conclusions about the family situation Ian's current head teacher drew particular attention to the 'fact' that Ian's parents were only co-operative on the surface: 'Mum was initially co-operative . . . and Mr Greaves was likewise quite co-operative until the decision was made to statement . . . . After that they opted out and didn't contact me.' Mrs Greaves, however, saw things differently, saying of the head teacher: 'She seemed to be assessing me rather than Ian . . . it's like she's shifting the blame on to me . . . she used to speak to me like I was a really bad mother. I used to come home in tears.'

Ian's teachers found some support for their view of the family situation from a community nurse who tried to work with the family. 'She thinks there's evidence of sexual abuse: soiling, language, and sexually overt behaviour.' In addition, the nurse supported the claim of uncooperativeness on the part of the Greaves, suggesting that in meetings with herself they had acted as if they had something to hide. 'On the occasions of visiting home I have felt most unwelcome and am therefore limited in the intervention I can provide.' In consequence, the community nurse recommended that a meeting with social services would be helpful to alert them to the dynamics of this family and to advise them that 'as professionals we were anxious that we had not managed to engage and intervene within the family and explore deficits in the parenting role'.

Following this report a meeting was held with social services. Mrs Greaves was invited to attend but was asked to wait outside while the professionals had a preliminary discussion of the case. Mrs Greaves observed that

> All different people went into the meeting – the health visitor, the doctor, teachers – but I couldn't go in. When I was allowed in, the child abuse officer was in the chair and he told me that his [Ian's] behaviour was the behaviour of a child who was sexually abused. They said they were not saying it was, but it was the behaviour. I went home in tears. They asked me to take the children for a full medical. I didn't want to but I was frightened they would think it was true, so I let them do it. I felt because they couldn't come up with anything else they brought this up to show it was something at home.

From the perspectives of both professionals and parents the attempt to build a co-operative framework had broken down. According to the professionals, the breakdown happened because the parents were responsible for Ian's special needs. Consequently, co-operation was defined by the professionals in terms that allowed them, in the words of the community nurse, to 'intervene within the family and explore deficits in the parenting role'. The parents were expected to accept the authority of the professionals even though there was little evidence to support their judgement. The parents' sense of disempowerment by this stage was almost total. Co-operation with the professionals would have required them to accept the framework within which Ian's needs had been cast by the professionals. In other words, co-operation would have meant acceptance that their own deficits as parents had created Ian's needs. On the other hand, refusal to co-operate would have been perceived by the professionals as reinforcing the latter's initial perceptions of the problem.

A problem/needs discourse is frequently established at an early stage, and, as we see here, because parents lack information about and access to the informal structures through which this discourse is established, they may find it almost impossible to challenge the assumptions made by professionals which underly it. It is this power to set the parameters of any discourse with parents that facilitates or inhibits parental involvement and control over the decision-making process. For instance, conceptualizing emotional and behavioural difficulties in terms of parental inadequacy or family breakdown has implications for how the role of parents in the assessment is then perceived. These perceptions legitimize the decision-making of professionals and mask the interests that lie behind those decisions; interests which are not necessarily made explicit during the assessment, and which may not consciously influence the practice of individual professionals.

PROFESSIONAL INTERVIEWS: FACT-FINDING AND DECISION-MAKING

Many professionals assume the primary purpose of their interviews with parents to be that of increasing the range and depth of information available to assist with decision-making, whether those decisions are to be made by the professionals themselves or by parents in partnership with professionals. In reality, however, the interview may be a far from neutral event (Armstrong *et al.* 1991). Burgess (1984) has drawn attention to the effects of interviewer characteristics on the data collection process. Gender, personal experience, age, social status, race and ethnicity may each 'create an immediate impression of the interviewer and will in part place limits on the roles that an interviewer may adopt' (Burgess 1984: 105). Moreover, the process by which an interviewer elicits information from an interviewee may become part of the client's perception of the interview's purpose. Indeed, the interview may itself impose behaviour as well as communicate information (Watzlawick *et al.* 1967). This can be illustrated by the different ways in which an interviewee might respond to differences in interview style. For instance, a child who, either correctly or incorrectly, perceives from the interviewer's manner that the interview has a disciplinary purpose is likely to respond differently to a child who perceives it to be a game. Interviewees' beliefs about how they are perceived by an interviewer may also significantly affect responses to questions during the interview.

Kuhn (1962) has argued that interviews may be analysed in terms of three component parts: participants' anticipations, including expectations about the purpose of the interview and the roles of those taking part; the interaction occurring within the interview setting itself; and the outcome or 'consensual termination' of the interview. This model is based on an interactionist perspective which emphasizes how the different interpretations people give to concepts and events arise from social relationships between them (Blumer 1962, 1969; Mead 1934). Thus: *'Meaning* refers to the fact that something *stands for* something else. . . . The person using symbols knows their meaning and uses them to communicate to others' (Charon 1979: 40–1). Through social interaction a consensus is reached about the use of symbols in that interaction. The professional interview may be seen not only as an aid to the identification of needs but also as a forum in which the needs of a child, as well as the needs of other participants, are negotiated. These negotiations can involve all participants acting in good faith!

The manipulation of the way other people see a particular situation is a common feature of social life, as is the attempt to manipulate how others see us in those situations (Goffman 1959). The participants in a professional interview are no different in this respect. The manipulation of expectations is concerned with the attempt to establish shared meanings that fit the objectives different participants hope to realize. The objectives of interviewer and interviewee may vary as may the meaning that is actually attributed to those objectives. Although there may be some common ground, the purpose of the interview is by no means established in advance. This depends upon more detailed negotiation within the interview itself. None the less, each participant may take steps to influence the anticipations of the other(s). Participants may communicate messages about their own role and how they perceive the roles of others in advance of any meeting between them. These messages may relate to the status, power and rights of different participants. Moreover, the formal roles of participants (that is, the role of psychologist, teacher, parent, doctor and so on) may also convey accumulated cultural messages about the owner-ship of knowledge and expertise, and about the power to control information and define 'needs'.

The choice of interview location itself (and who makes that choice) may be made with a particular purpose in mind. It may also reinforce client expectations of its purpose even where the professional perceives the client's role quite differently. On one occasion in the study the Education Office was chosen by a psychologist as the venue for an interview with a child who had been excluded from school and his parents. The psycholo-gist was aware that the school was seen by the parents as a site of conflict, and he therefore believed that the Education Office would be seen as a more 'neutral territory'. In another case the psychologist saw parents in their own home because he assumed they would be 'likely to be more relaxed on home ground'. A different psychologist was concerned that home visits might be seen by parents as intimidating, making them feel that their households were under inspection. Interestingly, none of the psychologists in this study appeared to be concerned by the fact that in almost every case it was they who made the decision about the time and venue of meetings. Psychologists were, however, far more willing to make concessions to their teacher clients on this point – most interviews with children and parents taking place in school so that teachers could be involved without causing them any great inconvenience. Parents, on the other hand, were expected to fit their arrangements around these visits to school.

An example of this occurred where a psychologist arranged for a meeting with parents to take place in school because he believed that these parents had a positive and trusting relationship with the staff at the school. This was true and was confirmed in a subsequent interview with the mother. None the less, she confided that she had found the prospect of an interview with the psychologist at the school to be a source of great anxiety: 'I thought he [her son] was in trouble at school.' Her sense of powerlessness in this situation was reinforced further by the circumstances of the invitation to attend the interview. It seemed to be assumed that she had nothing else to do in her life but to await being beckoned by professionals. On arriving home from work she found a hand-delivered letter from the school. 'The biggest shock was that there was a letter behind the door to say that the psychologist wanted to see me at 2.30 p.m. and it was 3.30 p.m. when I got in.'

Of the cases observed in this study, on only two occasions did parents make choices about interview venues. In respect of one of these the psychologist did not turn up for the meeting and sent no apologies. In the second case, however, a parent who wished to make 'serious allegations' concerning the way her son had been treated by his school insisted that the psychologist visit her at home at a time convenient to herself. In doing so she reinforced her expectation that the psychologist would act as her adviser and advocate.

NEGOTIATING PERSPECTIVES WITHIN THE INTERVIEW

Interviews with educational psychologists revealed that they were generally aware of their responsibilities towards different clients and aware also that the interests of these different clients were not always compatible. One psychologist, for instance, commented, that

> The major client is the child but it is necessary to look at the wider context, to take account of the needs of the teachers and other children. Sometimes teachers fall out with psychologists because they think we're not concerned with their needs.

For another psychologist it was the emphasis upon the facilitation of consensus or, put another way, the management of conflict, that made the 1981 Act procedures so attractive: 'I find the '81 Act very easy to work with because it does not ask me to define a problem but rather to deal with it as defined by the circumstances of the case.' This psychologist conceptualized his role in a way that recognized the constraints that the perspectives of others placed on the type of interventions available to him. Yet, by recognizing these constraints, he felt able to enter into negotiations with other participants in the assessment about the child's needs in ways that did not make his intervention entirely reactive. Precisely because he did not feel constrained by a requirement to use 'clinical' criteria in identifying children's needs he believed himself better able to influence the perceptions of others.

In mediating between conflicting perspectives psychologists in the study tried to get each participant to see the point of view of the others. This may facilitate agreement. It may also provide participants with the opportunity to re-examine what their own needs really are. Yet this can place great pressure on psychologists. There may also be times when, in seeking compromises between parties who are in conflict, the psychologist interprets what is being said in the interview in terms of the outcome that he or she is seeking.

In addition, interviewees may themselves seek to negotiate the psychologist's perception of an appropriate outcome during the interview.

Armstrong and Galloway (1992b) have argued that the perceptions of professionals such as educational psychologists about the nature of a professional relationship can vary from client to client and from session to session with each client. Even within a single session the nature of this relationship may undergo changes as meanings are negotiated and the professional responds to client expectations of the professional's role. The nature of these negotiations can be seen in a series of interviews between a psychologist and the parents of a child for whom residential education was being recommended.

George

George's teachers referred him to the Schools' Psychological Service when he was 9 years old. They were concerned about his behaviour in school and about the reports they had heard of his behaviour out of school. There had been a history of conflict between the school and George's parents, and the teachers believed these parents to be inadequate and responsible for many of the problems George was presenting in class. For their part, George's parents acknowledged that their family situation was stressful due to overcrowding in their home and the unemployment of George's father. They were anxious to receive help from the authorities but suspicious of the school and other professionals from the LEA who, they believed, wanted to remove George from his home.

The psychologist met Mr and Mrs Short on four occasions. During these interviews different aspects of George's needs were discussed, along with the needs of his parents and teachers. From the beginning the parents made their position clear: 'I don't think he's any worse than other kids – he's picked on by the school.' They argued that, because of the attitude of his teachers both to George and to the family generally, things had got so bad in his present school that he no longer had any chance of success there. They wanted him to be moved to another primary school and informed the psychologist that they had already applied to the head teacher of a nearby school for admission.

In the psychologist's first interview with these parents the latter, having confidence in the role of the psychologist as their advocate, expressed concern about the difficulties they had with George and were open about their perceptions of the dynamics of their family:

Psych.:   How is he at home?
Mrs Short: It's his brothers who carry on all the time. They pick on
              George. Michael has always been bad. [Michael is a

	year older than George and attends the same primary school. Andrew is a year younger and attends a residential school for children with moderate learning difficulties.]
Mr Short:	Michael went to live with his own dad but his dad couldn't cope. Since he's come home he's been a lot worse. He's taken it out on us because his dad didn't want him.
Psych.:	George has been in trouble with the police. Can you tell me about that?
Mrs Short:	I'm sick of calling the police out. We've tried to frighten him.
Psych.:	Have you had any contact with the social services?
Mrs Short:	No I don't want to have anything to do with them. I was going to put them into voluntary care to frighten them a bit, but I've talked to one or two people and they've said that if I do then it's really hard to get them back. . . . I hit Michael once and reported it myself. I just wanted some help, but I wish I hadn't now because I'm worried about him being taken off me.

Whereas, at the outset of this interview, the psychologist adopted a 'consultancy' model allowing the parents to express their concerns and seek expert advice, later in the interview this changed to a 'child protection' model as the psychologist interpreted these concerns as supporting the views of George's teachers that his needs would be best met in a residential school for children with emotional and behavioural difficulties. Consequently, when Mr Short suggested that it might be a good idea for both George and themselves if they could have a break away from each other the needs of the parents were used by the psychologist to legitimize her recommendation of a special school placement.

Mr Short:	There used to be a place in Scotland where kids could go to give parents a break. I don't know if there's anything like that round here. You've got to think of the kids as well – they've never had any holidays.
Psych.:	I'll try to make some enquiries about holidays. I do feel George will need some special schooling – he's not getting what he needs. Not because of anything to do with the school but he needs special help. What I'm trying to do at this stage is get your views. What I think we ought to do for any child getting a special education.

> We need to cover the paperwork. I think we should think about your feelings. Let's try and get you some help for you and the family.

The psychologist then explained in detail the statementing procedures, concluding with the information that a proposed statement would be sent to the parents, and at that stage:

> You can say whether or not you are happy with it and suggest any changes. No one is going to say George should go to another school until you are happy. You will be able to visit the school and see what you think. What we'll do now is set the process in motion.

It is interesting that at no stage in this interview did the parents agree even to consider George's placement in a residential special school. The decision to commence the statementing procedures was eventually made by default. Their acquiescence with the *psychologist's decision* to commence statementing arose from their belief that the psychologist was acting in the interests of the family. Yet it did not imply that they would be willing to accept this advice. The subtle, yet important, change in the model adopted by the psychologist had not been identified by the parents during the interview. They were not aware that George's special needs had been identified as arising from their own inadequacy as parents and that their own anxieties about their family situation and needs had been used to justify the proposal being put forward. Yet there is no reason to believe that this had been a deliberate ploy on the part of the psychologist to confuse and mislead the parents. To this extent the psychologist was similarly unaware of the subtle change in the professional role she was adopting in the interview with the Shorts. The confusion of both parties over the role of the psychologist was reflected in their different perception of what had been decided in the interview. The psychologist sent a memorandum to the LEA, in which she stated: 'I feel that George would benefit from placement in a residential school for pupils with emotional and behavioural problems. Mr and Mrs Short would be happy with a weekly boarding place.' When interviewed by the researcher shortly after their meeting with the psychologist, Mrs Short reaffirmed her opposition to George being placed in a residential school: 'I couldn't handle George at weekends if he was away all week.'

By their next meeting with the psychologist the Shorts' perception of the role of the psychologist had changed, and they saw her as acting in the interests of the school and the LEA. The psychologist, however, was unaware of this change in the parents' perception of her and assumed that the 'consensus' reached in the previous meeting still prevailed. Thus, she began the interview by stating her perception of that consensus:

Psych.:   Last time I saw you we felt that we should be looking at some kind of school with weekly boarding.

Mrs Short immediately responded that she did not want George put into residential school but rather wanted him to be allowed to change to a different mainstream primary school:

Mrs Short: We've been waiting for 1 year and 4 months to get him into another primary school.
Psych.:   That's where you would like him to go?
Mrs Short: Yes.

At this stage the differences between the perspectives of psychologist and parents are much more explicit than they had been in the previous interview. In response to this the psychologist modified her previous position. A new consensus was sought which did not entail any commitment to a particular outcome but which kept the psychologist's preferred outcome at the centre of negotiations between herself and parents rather than the parents' own preferred option of an alternative mainstream placement.

Psych.:   One possible school would be a weekly boarding – if you visited there would be no guarantee.
Mr Short: To be honest with you we have one child already at one of these schools and when he comes home he's a lot worse.
Psych.:   What I suggest we do – nothing's going to be decided today – I can arrange for you to have a look at one of the weekly residential schools . . . at this stage we're saying let's look.
Mrs Short: That's OK.

Thus an agreement appeared to have been reached.

The third interview came after the parents had visited a residential school and was very different in character from the previous interviews. Their main concern in this interview was that George's behaviour had been deteriorating rapidly over the twelve months of the assessment and yet during that time no help had been provided either in the school or at home. In the absence of any alternative being made available Mr Short was now willing to consider a residential school placement for George because

He's a handful, but now he's very upset now he knows – he's been for
a medical and he's very upset. Since his medical he's been crying every
morning saying his brother is glad he's going away. . . . Its not nice to
be taken away from your parents but we've got to try everything. . . .
We've got to think about it but I don't want him to end up getting into
a lot more trouble when he gets older.

By the fourth and final interview the parents had resigned themselves
to accepting the psychologist's recommendation. 'He's being picked on
by his teachers but something has to be done, he's getting older.' Moreover, they felt that, whilst sending him away might help his teachers, it
was unlikely to be of any help to them. Indeed their experience of the
deterioration in the behaviour at home of George's brother Andrew since
his placement in a residential school was seen by them as strong evidence
against the decision that had been taken.

The negotiations taking place over this series of interviews illustrate
how the role of parents in decision-making may be restricted to identifying
those aspects of the child's behaviour that fit or do not fit with the views
of professionals. But parents are not marginalized because professionals
deliberately exclude them from the decision-making process. In George's
assessment his parents were closely involved at each stage of decision-
making. From the psychologist's perspective it was the parents who made
the decision to send George to a residential school and that decision could
not have been made without their full agreement. Yet in practice they were
denied the opportunity to influence the way in which George's needs were
conceptualized by the psychologist. Moreover, they lacked the power to
negotiate on equal terms with the professionals about the interrelationship
between the needs of *all* participants in the assessment. The agenda for
negotiations between psychologist and parents in this case was set by the
psychologist on the basis of her perception of her own role as representing
the interests of child and teacher clients.

NEGOTIATING OUTCOMES

From an interactionist perspective, consensus over the meaning of symbols is negotiated in the interaction between participants. It is important,
however, to draw a distinction between an agreement between participants
about the desirability of particular substantive outcomes and a consensus
in respect of the framework of assumptions within which those decisions
are taken.

It could be argued that the consensus which existed with regard to the desirability of a residential school placement for George was very shallow. At various stages in the negotiations between psychologist and parents a consensus did appear to be achieved. This was certainly the psychologist's view. Yet, subsequently, George's parents continued to iterate strong arguments in favour of an outcome very different from the one that had been 'agreed'. The apparent consensus masked an underlying conflict of perspective between parents and psychologist. Even when the final decision was accepted by Mr and Mrs Short there were grounds for scepticism about the extent to which this agreement reflected a genuine consensus. From the psychologist's perspective it was a decision they wanted to take from the very beginning. Her role, as she saw it, had been to facilitate the decision 'they really want to make'. From the parents' perspective the decision reflected their resignation to the outcome rather than consensus about its desirability:

Mrs Short: As far as I'm concerned they give up too soon.
Mr Short: The way they were talking at that meeting George is going to a residential school [but] it's going to make him worse.

The experience of these parents during the earlier assessment of their younger son Andrew had not made them better able to resist the pressure they felt being exerted on them by the professionals. Reflecting on her level of involvement in Andrew's assessment Mrs Short said: 'We didn't get much to do with Andrew's assessment. I didn't want him to go to a residential school at all.'

The real consensus arrived at between professionals and parents in George's assessment was a consensus over who had the power to make decisions. As was argued in the previous section, when the actual dialogue of the first interview is analysed, a clear difference of opinion between parents and psychologist can be identified. Yet the psychologist confidently, and in good faith, asserted that an agreement had been reached. The parents took a very different view but the professionals were none the less seen as decision-makers. When Mrs Short was asked by the researcher about the outcome of this meeting she was unclear, because 'I haven't been told'.

CONCLUSION

Clashes of perspective between parents and psychologist, and the way in which these differences are resolved, cannot be seen in isolation from actual and perceived relationships of power. In George's case his parents were more aware of this than the psychologist. Whilst the latter saw her role as facilitating the participation of parents in decision-making, the latter saw their participation as merely legitimizing the decision-making of the psychologist. 'We've come to our own conclusions about what's going on. They want him out.'

The assessment was initiated at the request of the school when George was referred as an 'urgent case' because of problems in school arising from circumstances at home. By making the referral the school set the agenda for the assessment. The willingness of George's parents to participate in the assessment required them to accept that agenda as the starting point for future negotiations about the nature of George's needs. From the psychologist's perspective there were also problems in the school. She was aware of and sympathetic to the pressures staff in the school perceived themselves to be under because of the 'difficult' neighbourhood in which the school was situated. She also acknowledged that an additional complication in George's case was the fact that she believed his class teacher to be 'the worst teacher in the school'. Yet a discourse of needs had been established in this case at an early stage. The main feature of this discourse was that George's needs were conceptualized in terms of his teachers' perceptions of their own needs and, in particular, the threat they saw George as presenting to order and discipline within the school. The disempowerment of these parents in the decision-making process arose in a significant way because of their participation as partners in the assessment.

The opportunities parents have for expressing alternative interpretations of events and exploring the implications of these in their discussions with professionals is very much dependent upon how professionals conceptualize 'needs'. Unless professionals in general, and psychologists in particular, are able and willing to provide parents with a conceptual framework within which they can articulate different ways of understanding their child's needs, parent–professional partnership is likely to lead inevitably to the construction of a consensus which disempowers parents. Yet, as has been argued here, there may be significant factors that constrain psychologists and other professionals from offering such a framework to parents.

Chapter 4

Involving children in the assessment of special educational needs

Barton and Meighan's (1979) view that the pupil's perspective was one of the most under-researched areas in education is as true today as it was at that time. During the 1980s and 1990s, apart from a small number of notable exceptions (see, for example, Wade and Moore 1993), there has continued to be little interest shown by researchers in what children themselves have to say about their educational experiences. The fragmentation of political and social life under the guise of a radical neo-liberalism, together with financial cutbacks and recession, have shifted attention far away from those radical critiques of schooling which started from a desire to understand the learner's experience (Hargreaves 1967; Lacey 1970; Willis 1977; Woods 1979). Their place has now largely been taken by the instrumental concerns of a struggling economy (Giroux 1983).

Despite this there is a small number of educational researchers, some of them influenced by child-care developments outside of the education system, who have expressed concern about what can happen when children are *not* listened to. This has led those researchers to an interest in techniques for gaining access to children's thinking and involving children in the decision-making processes in areas that affect their futures (Davie 1991; Davie and Galloway, in press; Gersch 1987, 1992). Yet the issues raised by these attempts to take children seriously are far from straightforward. It will be argued in this chapter that a central difficulty professionals face in gaining access to children's thinking in these contexts arises from the failure to contextualize professional practice within a theoretical framework that shows the relationship between the construction of childhood identities (including deviant identities) and the social structures within which they occur.

GAINING ACCESS TO THE CHILD'S PERSPECTIVE

The reasons why children commonly play a subordinate role within assessment procedures under the 1981 Education Act are likely to be varied and complex. However, professionals are faced with a clinically difficult task in gaining access to children's perspectives and therefore maximizing the contribution children can make to the assessment. These difficulties are not confined to special needs assessments and can clearly be seen to occur across a whole range of adult–child interactions. Gaining access to children's perspectives requires skill in communicating meanings to children and understanding the meanings embedded in children's language and behaviour. It also requires an understanding of the nature of interactions between adults and children.

Interest in the interactions between professionals and children is not new. Psychiatrists concerned with issues about the validity and reliability of the interview as a tool of diagnostic assessment (Cox and Rutter 1976; Rutter and Graham 1968) have provided valuable evidence concerning the validity and reliability of interviewing styles and techniques and this has assisted the development of appropriate clinical methods for listening to children. These authors concluded that the interview with a child can be a valid and reliable tool for diagnosing childhood psychiatric disorders, particularly when used in conjunction with a wide range of other techniques. Yet they also emphasized the need for caution in the interpretation of interview data:

> A short psychiatric interview with a child was found to be a reasonably sensitive diagnostic instrument which could give rise to reliable and valid judgements on whether the child exhibited any psychiatric disorder. However, on the whole, individual ratings on specific aspects of behaviour proved to be less reliable than the overall psychiatric diagnosis. There were also marked differences in the reliability and usefulness of the various specific ratings.
>
> (Rutter and Graham 1968: 576)

Following upon the relatively recent public acknowledgement of the prevalence of child sexual abuse, concern about child welfare has led to fresh interest being shown in the problems involved in devising appropriate methods for gaining access to children's thinking and the validation of children's accounts of events (see, for example, the collection of essays on this subject in Bannister *et al.* 1990). One of the major issues that has been highlighted by recent child abuse inquiries is the importance of professionals adopting methods that take into account both the developmental status of the child and the individual differences between children. This emphasizes the need for professionals to be appropriately trained. Freeman (1990) has argued that the general inadequacy of training for professionals working with children is a serious impediment to the success of professional interventions with children in need. He maintains of professional intervention that

> Rarely does it penetrate into an understanding of child psychology. Too little insight into techniques of interviewing children is offered. Nor is this surprising given how inadequate a training is given to social workers and others whose daily task is to elicit from children what concerns them and what views they wish to express or get others to express on their behalf. The whole Cleveland episode is testimony to the ham-fisted way interviews, particularly the so-called 'disclosure' assessments, were conducted.
>
> (Freeman 1990: 34)

Where conceptual systems are imposed on children's accounts by adults these are likely to result in a distortion of the meanings used by children. Adult perceptions of children's beliefs and perspectives may be inadequate or even inaccurate unless grounded in the meanings used by children. Assumptions made by adults about the behaviour of children may lead to the rationality of children's actions being questioned and to their voices being disregarded 'in their own interests'. Thus the disempowerment of children may be reinforced by inappropriate methods of 'listening'.

INVOLVING PUPILS IN THE ASSESSMENT OF THEIR OWN SPECIAL EDUCATIONAL NEEDS

It is only very recently that concern has been expressed about the disadvantaged role of children in the procedures for assessing their special educational needs and arguments put forward demanding recognition of the unique perspective of the child as an authentic interpretation of the child's reality (Gersch 1987). Historically, children have not only been disenfranchised in the decision-making processes that directly affect them but they have also frequently been seen as no more than the property of their parents (Freeman 1987). Even now, despite increased public awareness of how children are made vulnerable by being denied a voice in decisions affecting their lives, the evidence of involvement remains patchy and the evidence of professional anxiety about how to enhance the child's role is plentiful. The Cleveland child-abuse case highlighted the pitfalls faced by professionals in their attempts to act in the interests of children; it also emphasized the consequences of ignoring child testimonies. Significantly, the report of the inquiry into this case recommended that professionals should always listen carefully to children and take what they say seriously, maintaining that 'the views and wishes of the child, particularly as to what should happen to him/her, should be taken into account by the professionals involved with their problems' (Butler-Sloss 1988: 245).

This recommendation followed the precedent set in the appeal court's judgment in the case of Gillick (1986), a case with major implications for the legal rights of children. In this case it was judged that, where a girl had the maturity and understanding to evaluate different courses of action, she could seek and be given contraceptive advice without the permission of her parents. Subsequently this principle has been generalized to the child's right to make decisions in many other areas. In particular, a more limited version of this principle has been given legislative authority in the 1989 Children Act. This legislation, for the first time, placed a statutory duty on those with responsibility for identifying children's needs to take account of 'the ascertainable wishes and feelings of the child concerned (considered in the light of his age and understanding)' (Children Act 1989, Section 1(1)).

Educational legislation has lagged some way behind the 1989 Children Act. Although some commentators have argued that the 1981 Education Act embodied a radical extension of consumer rights, by creating opportunities for parents to be involved in the assessment of their children's special educational needs, the Act is silent about the contribution of children themselves to the assessment process. The Department of Education and Science (DES 1989a), in its advice on assessments under the 1981 Education Act, nevertheless recommends that 'The feelings and perceptions of the child should be taken into account and the concept of partnership should wherever possible be extended to older children and young persons' (para. 21).

In view of these developments it is perhaps surprising to find that with regard to educational decision-making children remain very much the 'property' of their parents. For instance, the 1988 Education Reform Act implicitly rejects any claim children might have to be consumers of educational services by denying them the right to be consulted over the schools they will attend and the curriculum they will study. Indeed, Rosenbaum and Newell (1991) have argued that it is in respect of the child's role in educational decision-making that the United Nations Charter on the Rights of Children is most seriously disregarded in Britain today.

The 1993 Education Act does, for the first time, establish the principle that the child's views should be sought during an assessment of their special educational needs (Regulation 6). The Code of Practice on the Identification and Assessment of Special Educational Needs (DFE 1994), issued under the 1993 Education Act, has elaborated upon this by identifying the importance of involving children both on grounds of principle – 'children have the right to be heard, therefore should be encouraged to participate in decision-making about provision to meet their special educational needs' – and good practice – 'children have important and relevant information. Their support is crucial to the effective implementation of any individual education programme.' The inclusion of this statement of the importance of the child's role in the assessment has been widely applauded, but these general statements are not unproblematic and indeed may considerably oversimplify the difficulties encountered by professionals in gaining access to children's perspectives. Moreover, they may oversimplify the implications for the child of participation in an assessment.

Gersch, drawing on personal construct theory, has argued that psychological theory provides a strong rationale for giving children a more active role in their own assessments.

> People negotiate the world, interpreting what is experienced, and base their perceptions on their past experiences and anticipations. Within Personal Construct Theory people are seen as active participants and not passive recipients of external events. Each person creates his or her own experiential world, which includes events in the outside world, as well as thoughts, emotions and sensations. Additionally constructions are based upon memories, anticipations, hopes, fears and plans. In short, to understand the person one must understand his or her own construction of the world and the underlying bases of those constructions. Problems can arise when there is a mismatch between the person's own view of events and those of others. It is vital, therefore, to recognize and acknowledge that each person has their own unique and individual interpretation of the world.
>
> (Gersch 1987: 151)

Gersch goes on to discuss four projects on pupil involvement in assessments under the 1981 Education Act in which he has been involved. He argues that the success of these projects (judged on the criterion of the positive responses of pupils participating in them) illustrate that it is possible to increase the active involvement of some children in the assessment process by creating opportunities for the child to express a view of situations even though that view might be in conflict with that of his or her teachers. By adopting such techniques and involving the child, the origins of conflict can be better identified and consensus over the resolution of conflicts more easily obtained.

The case made by Gersch here for involving children in the assessment process (see also Gersch and Cutting 1985; Gersch *et al.* 1993), and more generally in planning and implementing whole school policy changes (Gersch and Noble 1991), is a strong one. Yet, it may still be questioned whether policies and procedures designed to ensure children's involvement in assessment and decision-making are sufficient to ensure their empowerment. The concept of 'power' is treated somewhat uncritically in this literature as it is in much of the literature on parent–professional partnerships. Conflict and its resolution are analysed in terms of the interactions between pupil and teacher alone without consideration being given to the context of that relationship within the social structure. Thus the resolution of conflict is seen as occurring simply through the willingness of participants to see each other's perspective. Understanding is seen as the basis of consensus yet the nature of the consensus is treated as unproblematic. A number of questions are begged by this formulation:

1 How might the way power is distributed contribute to the construction of a consensus between participants in a social event?

2 In what ways might negotiations between participants in a social event construct a distribution or redistribution of power in their relationship?

3 Are assumptions that the professional is *or should be* a neutral information seeker, or alternatively an advocate for the child, justifiable?

4 What 'social function' does the assessment process (whatever its outcome) play in the construction of particular identities for children, and how do interventions by professionals contribute to the construction of those identities?

5 To what extent is the professional able to hear what the child has to say when account has to be taken of the needs of other participants in the assessment process?

6 How does the child perceive the role of professionals in the assessment process, and in what circumstances might that perception be justified even though it differs from the professional's own perception of her or his role?

Professionals' interviews with children are critical social events. The 'event' will include the expectations that each party brings to the interview and, vicariously, the expectations of non-participants which, despite their absence, none the less limit and constrain the forms of consensus that it is possible to negotiate in the interview event itself. The distribution of status and power implicit in adult–child relationships is a good example of expectations that are culturally embedded in the interaction between participants in a social situation. It may be possible to renegotiate aspects of this relationship within the specific context of the interview between professional and child, but an implicit consensus about the relationship, derived from cultural expectations, may persist despite the intentions of those in culturally dominant roles explicitly to abrogate power and control over their social subordinates.

In examining the role of children in decision-making where decisions are made with or by professionals it is important to know how professionals go about the business of gaining access to children's perspectives. It is also important to understand what constraints, including cultural constraints, operate on both professionals and children to inhibit the involvement of children in that decision-making process. This suggests that attempts to communicate effectively with children in ways that empower them in the decision-making process require more than an appreciation of psychological techniques. The cultural and social processes underlying the decision-making process (and the child's role in it) and the construction of needs within that process must themselves be subjected to theoretical and empirical analysis.

'NEEDS' AND THE CONSTRUCTION OF CHILDHOOD IDENTITIES

A historical perspective

The concept of childhood is often taken for granted as if it were adequately described by reference to biological and developmental changes. It is a concept, however, that also has social and political significance. Disentangling the history of childhood, particularly as it developed before the nineteenth century, is highly problematic, not least because empirical data are extremely sparse. 'What is a child?' is a question that is not easily answered, and certainly the qualities attributed to children vary, often dramatically, from the perspective of one historical period to another. Many taken-for-granted twentieth-century western assumptions about childhood cannot be identified in earlier centuries or in different cultures.

Aries (1962) has maintained that the development of the modern concept of childhood was linked not to any notion of 'care' but rather to that of 'control'. Although Aries' thesis regarding the origins of the concept of childhood has been disputed (Pollock 1983), there is more general agreement that the modern conception of childhood was accompanied by an increasing strictness of discipline and supervision. A characteristic of child care in the twentieth century has been the willingness of the state to intervene in areas of life that had once been the sole domain of the family. Indeed, according to Aries, the development of the modern concept of childhood in western societies is inextricably linked to the development of the modern state. The involvement of the state in child control occurred in direct response to the resistance of the children of the poor throughout the nineteenth century to the training in discipline that was required by new forms of industrial production:

> unlike adults, they rarely belonged to institutions which depended on personal and collective discipline. They did, it is true, normally belong to family units, but it was the very weakness of the family, particularly among the very poor, which persuaded many observers to suggest schooling as a supplement or alternative to the family as an agent for disciplining and controlling the young.
>
> (Walvin 1982: 185)

The role of the state in the construction of childhood identities

The move towards a centralized system of control and discipline for the young, generated by modern forms of economic and social organization, has led to a larger role being played by the state in relation to child care. Yet this picture of state intervention, drawn solely in terms of control, is misleading precisely because it is so unidimensional. The role of the state and its institutions in the construction of social identities through childhood is likely to differ in respect of different social groups. An understanding of the different social experiences of children from different social classes and subgroups would provide valuable clues to indicate how different childhoods operate either to facilitate the accumulation and control of knowledge by socially dominant groups or the reproduction of those forms of social order required for mass economic production.

Although the state may play a central role in the reproduction of 'knowledge power' and 'labour power' in capitalist societies, an account of the state and its agencies in these terms alone is an oversimplification. It takes no account of the processes by which individuals and groups construct and internalize their experiences in the context of negotiations over what that 'reality' will be. Moreover, childcare and educational policies do not operate merely as a function of social reproduction; they contain tensions and contradictions creating the conditions in which different social groups may contend for power in their day-to-day lives.

Fox Harding (1991) has suggested a fourfold classification of the value perspectives associated with the tension between care and control in the twentieth century. The first, which she calls the 'laissez-faire' or 'patriarchy' perspective, holds that the role of the state should be minimal and that the power residing in the family should not be disturbed except in extreme circumstances. The second, which she calls the 'state-paternalism and child protection' perspective, is associated with the growth in state intervention in welfare and the belief that state intervention to protect and care for children is legitimate. The modern 'defence of the birth family and parents' rights' is a third perspective, which again views state intervention as legitimate but only in so far as it supports the family. From this perspective parents are often seen as the victims of state action. The fourth perspective identified by Fox Harding is the 'children's rights' perspective. This perspective sees children as independent persons to be freed from adult oppression by being granted a more adult status.

Although elements of these perspectives are associated with different political positions Fox Harding maintains that they are by no means exclusively linked to distinct political positions. The extent to which one or all of these perspectives have been prominently reflected in legislation and policy at any one time in the history of child care in Britain has varied. However, Fox Harding argues that policy is often constructed as a pragmatic response reflecting aspects of each of these different and often conflicting positions.

The processes involved in the construction of this 'pragmatic response' are not spelled out by Fox Harding who, for the most part, treats them as abstract value-positions with an influence upon policy-making. The origins of these value-positions in social interests is largely unexplored. She argues that there is no clear or logical association between any of the value perspectives she identifies and particular political positions or interests. On the other hand, there is a heavy social investment in the care and socialization of the young. The differences and conflicts between different perspectives, therefore, may be seen as reflecting debates about the most efficient way of achieving that and about the resources that should be committed to it. At this level, however, any debate about the 'rights' of individuals and groups with special needs, or with responsibilities for those with special needs, avoids more analytical questions about the origin of those needs: who has them, how they are constructed and whose interests are served by the ways in which they are defined?

Resistance, consensus and reproduction in schools

Through individual and collective agency people negotiate (by action as well as through discourse) the conditions of their own reality and the reality of others. The outcome of these negotiations may legitimate certain aspects of the existing forms of social relations or result in changes to those relations. The reproduction of existing social forms is not an inevitable part of any consensus reached. This reflects the fact that the struggle for consensus is also a struggle for power. The need for dominant groups to forge a consensus in order to maintain effectively their position of control contains within it the conditions for subordinate groups to contest that power.

The nature of this process was illustrated by Willis (1977) in his study of conflict in a working-class secondary school. In a subsequent discussion of Willis's study, Apple has argued that it

> demonstrated that rather than being places where culture and ideologies are imposed on students schools are the sites where these things are produced . . . they are produced in ways that are filled with contradictions and by a process that is itself based on contestation and struggle.
> (1982: 26)

Willis (1977) showed how the 'lads' resisted the values that the school attempted to transmit by constructing their own counter-culture with its roots in their own working-class communities. Their rejection of the school's values and the emphasis placed by the school upon the superiority of mental labour, Willis argues, was based upon recognition of how the ideology of the education system was operating to pacify and disempower them. From their perspective the working-class culture of their families and communities suggested a reality that was more convincing than that suggested by the values of the school.

Ironically, rejection of 'mental labour' by the 'lads' stemmed from an 'intellectual' critique of the role of the school in their lives. The fact that this critique was not fully articulated does not detract from the point that their resistance to schooling originated out of their rejection of the relevance of its values to their own lives. Culture and ideologies are not simply imposed on pupils by schools; thus the process by which schools reproduce social forms contain the conditions for articulating opposition to those forms (Apple 1982).

Resistance and consensus in the construction of special educational needs

The expansion of special educational provision may be seen as reflecting humanitarian concerns for the care of children whose disadvantaged lives limit their educational opportunities. This view of special education identifies its growth within a framework of expanding opportunities. In contrast to this humanitarian perspective, it has been argued that the expansion of special education actually reflects structural changes within society. Tomlinson, for instance, in looking at the construction of illiteracy as a special need, pointed out how

> technological advance has permanently displaced the need for manual labour. Until relatively recently, the lower-class Johnnies who could not read functioned very well as manual labourers. Now, achievements in ordinary education (which are based on reading) are crucial to gaining any kind of employment or income above subsistence level. Those who are defined as unable or unwilling to participate in ordinary education are likely to remain partially or permanently unemployed and to be destined for a life of relative dependence and – however humanitarian – of more social control. . . . However, such a society needs to rationalise the resulting 'uselessness' of many of its citizens. Special education is fast becoming a means of legitimating a labour crisis by dealing with the 'useless'.
>
> (Tomlinson 1988: 48)

The latter position suggests that the conceptualization of educational failure, disturbing behaviour and disablement in terms of humanitarian concern serves to contain opposition to the structures that are responsible for the creation of those categories. Humanitarian conceptualizations of 'need' legitimate the disempowerment of those identified as 'needy' precisely because the ideology of special educational needs denies people so labelled the 'equal opportunity' to negotiate a definition of their needs in terms of their political and social origins.

Yet the formation of a consensus about the nature of special educational needs is important if the social interests which it serves are to be legitimated. The character of this consensus lies in its recognition of people's genuine needs whilst treating the circumstances in which these needs are constructed as unproblematic. This ideological framework provides the context within which negotiations about how needs are to be identified and met takes place. The child's own involvement in this negotiation is likely to be contradictory.

On the one hand, negotiations over a child's needs take place within a framework over which the child has little or no control. At a formal level this is to be found in the framework of the 1981 Education Act. At an informal level this framework is found in the cultural forms which are reproduced through social institutions (Bourdieu and Passeron 1977). A consequence of participation for the child is that it serves to legitimate that framework (negotiation takes place over whether the child's behaviour, and so on, meets the criteria employed within this framework, not over the validity of the framework). In this sense the child's participation may contribute to the construction of what Goffman (1968) has referred to as 'spoiled identity'. Yet, as so far drawn, this picture assumes the child to be passive in the assessment, whereas in practice the child might articulate participation in terms of resistance to what the label is believed to stand for. Moreover, in practice, negotiations over children's needs may incorporate negotiations about the needs of a much wider group of people. If the assessment is a site for the negotiation of *those* needs, then the conflicting perspectives of different participants in respect of their own needs may enable the child to resist the labelling process and influence the outcome of the assessment in ways that are self-empowering. This may occur through formal provisions for consultation but may occur also through more informal negotiations and action.

Aronowitz and Giroux have suggested that one of the weaknesses of critical theory has been its concentration upon forms of resistance as political acts at the expense of an analysis of how opposition may itself reinforce domination: 'when resistance is discussed, its contradictory nature is usually not analysed seriously, nor is the contradictory consciousness of the students and teachers treated dialectically' (1985: 103).

The nature of the process referred to here is different from Goffman's (1968) notion of 'spoiled identities'. Whereas for Goffman 'spoiled identities' arise from the internalization by the labelled person of the label, the question raised by critical theory should be that of how opposition and resistance to the labelling process may themselves reproduce the forms of control that are resisted.

The notion of 'resistance' is one that is susceptible to romanticization, and this can be seen in some of the research from a critical theory perspective – all resistances being represented as self-empowering political action. Methodologically, this is reflected in a tendency, that can be seen in Willis's work, to accept uncritically how subjects perceive and represent themselves. Theoretically, this has inhibited an analysis of how resistance is transformed into the self-empowerment of subordinate groups. Willis (1977), for instance, appears to assume that the 'lads' are empowered by their resistance alone, yet it might be argued that their action, divorced from any explicit political articulation, functions to reinforce their political disempowerment. The conditions under which resistance is politically articulated to effect social change is unexplored. The other side of this coin is that there is no analysis of how individuals internalize 'deviant' identities through the forms that their resistance takes – in other words, how strategies of resistance may themselves, in certain circumstances, isolate and contain opposition. It is towards a better understanding of this that we must direct our efforts.

CONCLUSION

This chapter began by pointing to the neglect of children's perspectives in the literature on education. In recent years some attention has started to focus upon those children seen to be most vulnerable. It might be questioned whether this higher profile has led to significant changes in the rights of children or indeed to greater protection being afforded to them. Current interest may, in practice, merely reflect the fact that previously taboo issues have begun to enter the public domain.

There is evidence (the 1989 Children Act being the most obvious example) of greater official emphasis being placed on the child's point of view in matters affecting him or her. The evidence is less convincing in other areas, including education. There is a rhetoric of participation and partnership surrounding the 1981 Education Act, and this has been supported by advice from the DES on the implementation of the Act. The 1981 Act itself says nothing about the contribution of children to decision-making in the assessment although, somewhat belatedly, the 1993 Education Act has brought assessment practices in line with duties placed upon LEAs and their advisers by the 1989 Children Act.

Empowering children in the decision-making processes that affect them in assessments raises complex clinical issues. Sensitivity and skill are required, and evidence has been discussed suggesting that frequently both these qualities are lacking in professionals' work with children. There are practitioners who do take the child's perspective seriously and in doing so make systematic attempts to give children a voice. The work of Gersch has been significant in this respect because it has treated the child's perspective as equal in importance to that of adults in seeking the resolution of conflict. Yet it has been argued in this chapter that, despite the advances represented by this work, it has underanalysed the concept of 'power'. By contrast, it has been argued here, that the importance of the child's perspective lies in its relevance to an elaboration of the complex ways by which power is reproduced in society.

The concept of 'childhood' should not be seen simply in biological or developmental terms. It also has a social and political significance. In modern capitalist societies that significance is closely related to the role of the state and its institutions (including the education system) as sites of conflict in the reproduction of social forms. The concept of 'consensus' has been identified along with that of 'conflict' as central to an understanding of this process of reproduction. It has been argued that the reproduction of power and control in society is not occasioned mechanistically through social institutions such as the education system but rather through conflict and the forms of consensus by which conflict is resolved. This involves contradictory processes. Dominant groups maintain their dominance by negotiating forms of consensus about the needs of subordinate groups that reflect their own interests. However, this process contains possibilities for subordinate groups to articulate and negotiate alternative constructions of their needs and interests, leading to greater empowerment in particular aspects of their lives.

It has been suggested in this chapter that the conflict between humanitarian and control perspectives on the role of special education make this an important site for analysing the relationship between conflict and consensus in the construction and reproduction of needs and power. Yet most previous research into the processes of special education, including that which has sought to investigate how special education serves to reproduce and legitimate aspects of the social structure, has chosen to ignore the child's perspective on these processes. This neglect means that little is known about the experiences of those participants who stand at the centre of the special education system. This alone would justify research to elaborate that perspective, but it has been argued in this chapter that it is *only* through understanding the interactions involving the child and the meanings attributed by children to those interactions that it is possible to construct an adequate theoretical account of the processes involved.

Chapter 5

Children's perspectives on assessment

It is somewhat ironic that in the debates that have taken place over educational values, from the 1944 Education Act to the 1988 Education Reform Act, from Plowden (CACE 1967) to Choice and Diversity (DFE 1992), from the Warnock Report (DES 1978) to the Code of Practice on the assessment of special educational needs (DFE 1994), there has been little concern with how children, as the direct consumers of such initiatives, view their benefits or experience their deficiencies. We live in a society where concerns about the education and welfare of children are seen as integral to the development and future prosperity of that society, and yet children are rarely consulted about what they want for their own futures or about their experience of the present. This neglect is not confined solely to politicians and policy makers. As was argued in Chapter 4, neglect of the child's perspective is commonly a sin of omission which characterizes the work of educational researchers. Neglect is insidious in that its outcome extends beyond mere disregard of those without a voice. Its significance lies in the way in which it imputes passivity to the child, suggesting that the child is powerless to effect change in the educational and social processes in which he or she is a participant. The silence of the child may then, perversely, be used to justify the paternalism which is itself a source of the child's disempowerment. This chapter attempts to probe beyond the silence, to consider how children themselves understand and make sense of the aims and outcomes of the procedures for assessing special educational needs and the consequences for them of the labels which these assessments place on them. In doing so it will draw on research undertaken by the author into the assessment of children identified as having emotional and behavioural difficulties.

In total, forty-seven children participated in this research (an additional nine children participated in the pilot study but not in the main study). This sample comprised three sub-samples. The first of these was a sample of seven children attending an off-site special unit for children with behavioural difficulties (Table 5.1). The second sub-sample was made up of eleven children attending two residential schools specializing in the education of children identified as having emotional and behavioural difficulties (Table 5.2). Collectively these samples are referred to as the 'retrospective' sample because the data source in each case was the child's retrospective account given in interview. The third sub-sample, referred to as the 'concurrent' sample, comprised twenty-nine children, the main stages of whose assessments were observed by the researcher (Table 5.3).

Table 5.1 Characteristics of unit sample

Age	Pupils	Months attending unit
5 or under	1	12
6–7	2	24, 24
8–9	3	12, 24, 30
10–11	1	42

Table 5.2 Characteristics of the residential schools sample

Age	Boys	Girls	Total
11–14	4	2	6
15 and over	4	1	5
Total	8	3	11

Table 5.3 Distribution of concurrent sample by age and gender

Age	Boys	Girls	Total
Under 7	6	1	7
7–11	6	1	7
12–14	11	1	12
15–16	2	1	3
Total	25	4	29

Collectively the accounts summarized in this chapter represent some 70 to 80 hours of interviews with children. Each child in the retrospective sample was interviewed in school over a period of approximately 30 to 45 minutes. With the exception of one child, children in the concurrent sample were interviewed on at least one occasion during the course of their assessment. In addition, observations were made of professionals' interviews with these children during the assessment. Prior to each interview it was explained to the child that the interview was taking place as part of a research project and that the researcher was not working for the school or the local authority. The confidentiality of the interview was emphasized and the children given an opportunity to decline participation in the research. Although no children refused permission one child did not wish to be interviewed and on three other occasions children made it clear that they did not want a particular line of questioning to continue. In these cases the children's wishes were respected. Details of the outcome in each of the cases in the concurrent sample are given in Table 5.4.

Table 5.4 Assessment outcomes

EBD residential special school	13
EBD day special school	4
MLD day special school	1
Additional support in mainstream	3
Reintegration supported by a statement	2
No action taken	3
Statementing procedures not completed	
before end of research	3
Total	29

The interviews followed a semi-structured design but the precise format varied depending upon the age of the child. Interviews with children in the concurrent sample focused more specifically on issues arising from observations made by the researcher during the assessment. However, areas common to both samples were explored as follows:

1   The child's perceptions of the reasons for assessment/placement;
2   The child's perception of the assessment process, including perceptions of the role of different professionals in that process;
3   The child's perception of their own involvement in the decision-making process;
4   The child's perception of their own needs and the extent to which these had been addressed by the assessment/placement;

5   The child's perception of the effects of the assessment/placement on their self-image and status within the family, peer group and community.

PERCEPTION OF THE REASONS FOR ASSESSMENT/PLACEMENT

All but two of the children in the unit sample had been attending the unit for two years or longer. It is not surprising, therefore, that their memory of the events leading to their placement were vague. Four children could offer no account at all of the reason for their placement. The events leading to the placement of children in the residential school samples were more recent, but the accounts these children gave also tended to be vague. None the less, the way in which children reconstruct events, and even their inability to remember them at all, is of interest because that reconstruction, however distorted, may have significant implications for how the child interprets their present experiences.

Each of the eleven children in the residential schools believed their behaviour had been a factor leading to their placement. One child stated that it was 'because I was not good enough', whilst another said that it was 'for messing about and giving cheek'. A third child gave a similar reason: 'It was probably because of my behaviour and cheek.' In these cases it was clashes with authority in school rather than difficulties at home that were given as the reason. One of the unit children said that 'I ran off from school. I thought the teachers were picking on me.' He said that following this he had returned to the school for five months but that on his return he had been told by a teacher that 'They just took me back while they were waiting for a place here [at the unit].'

Personality clashes with teachers or other children in school were cited by all eleven of the residential schoolchildren as a major factor leading to their final removal from mainstream school. One child, for example, stated that 'I didn't get on with any of the teachers there or anything. I got on with some of the lads but most of them hurted me.'

Most children in these interviews identified their experiences at school as the origin of their difficulties. Very few references were made to family problems as a factor leading to their placement. It is perhaps reasonable to assume, at least in respect of those children who had been placed in residential schools, that family circumstances had been a factor in the placement decision. Whether the children were reluctant to talk about this because of the sensitivity of the issues involved or whether they were genuinely unaware of its significance as a factor influencing the placement decision is something that can only be speculated about in the absence of more detailed information. Many of the children did acknowledge, however, that their families were under great pressure, and expressed concern that their own difficulties and problems in school might have added to those pressures. (Galloway in his study of *Schools and Persistent Absentees* (1985b), found that truants were similarly reluctant to identify home factors as the reason for the absenteeism from school but they did freely concede that stresses at home, such as parental illness, were relevant when questioned more generally about their families.)

Two children in the unit sample and four in the residential schools sample identified learning difficulties as a significant factor leading to their eventual placement in special education. Karen, for instance, said that she had to go to a residential school 'because I weren't so good with my school work and I didn't get on with the other kids.' Robert said that he 'came to the unit because I'm dyslexic. It means I read my words back to front.' Sean, whilst admitting to getting into trouble for fighting at his mainstream school, was none the less adamant that 'I got sent here [the unit] because of my reading, not because of my behaviour. . . . Dyslexia means you've got a short mind and can't read so well. Its like amnesia but you forget things.'

For many children in the concurrent sample difficulties in relationships at school were an on-going experience during the assessment. Eighteen children specifically identified problems with relationships in school as the reason why their assessment had been started. Gavin said that he had been sent to a residential school 'because I had a bad attitude in my last school'. Stephen said that he had been sent to residential school because 'my teachers couldn't handle me. I was giving them that much stick.' For Simon his placement in a special school was a consequence of his 'doing stuff I wasn't allowed to. I was putting glue on the teacher's chair and playing tricks on the head teacher.' James reported that after he was excluded from school 'They had to start [the assessment] because they had nowhere else for me to go.'

Two children in this sample also identified difficulties in their relationships with other members of their families as a reason why the assessment had been started. Interviews with staff at the schools suggested that a larger number of children than this had actually experienced problems at home, but these were the only children who made any explicit connection between family problems and the initiation of the assessment. One of these, Sean, was unhappy because he believed he had made big improvements in his behaviour at school yet the break-up of his parents' marriage and 'my mum's inability to manage me' led to his being placed initially in a social services assessment centre and later a residential special school: 'They treated me unfairly. It wasn't related to any events at school.' Bryan also saw conflicts at home as the prime reason for his assessment: 'It was not the school who wanted me to see a psychologist but my mother's suggestion. Personally I can't see anything wrong with me.'

Only four children in the concurrent sample identified learning difficulties as a reason for their assessments being initiated. Peter said that he had to go to a special unit because: 'I had problems in doing my work in a certain length of time. I couldn't cope and just weren't doing it. I was also getting aggravation from my teacher who was against me because my cousin had given her a lot of trouble.' Gavin, although accepting that it was his behaviour that had resulted in his being placed in a special school, none the less believed that children went to residential special schools when they had learning difficulties as well as behaviour problems: 'I couldn't go to a day school because I wasn't clever enough.' Michael saw the origin of his problems in school as the attitude of his teachers and peers towards his learning difficulties: 'I never got any attention. There was a lot of people aggravating me because I wasn't bright. I was more or less the thickest in the class and I used to smash out at them.'

PERCEPTIONS OF THE ASSESSMENT PROCESS

Interviews with children in the unit and the residential schools revealed that many were unaware of how decisions had been reached. A possible reason for this ignorance might have been that the professionals with responsibility for conducting assessments did little to inform children of those procedures and involve them in the decision-making process. These retrospective interviews do not allow such a claim to be tested. However plausible this interpretation might appear, it is perhaps over-simplistic. It is important to exercise caution in interpreting children's retrospective accounts. The fallibility of children's memories may affect the validity of the data reported here because of the time lapse between children's assessments and the research interviews (two or more years in respect of some of the children in the unit). This does not mean that the children's accounts are of no interest, only that they should not be accepted unconditionally as an accurate statement of events.

Four of the children in the unit could not remember anything about an assessment or meeting with a psychologist prior to their admission. One child (aged 7) thought that the decision had been taken by 'my taxi lady' because children were brought to the unit by taxi! For at least one of the unit children there was evidence from staff reports to corroborate the claim that no assessment had been undertaken by the LEA's schools' psychological service. Of the two remaining children, one said that he had been seen by 'a psychology teacher who was at the hospital', whilst the other said that before coming to the unit someone had come to his school to give him some tests: 'They had a funny name I can't pronounce.'

The children in the residential school sample, although vague about the purpose and procedures of the assessment, demonstrated greater awareness of having been 'assessed' prior to their placement. This is not very surprising given that these children were all older than the unit children and that they had been assessed formally under the provisions of the 1981 Act rather than informally.

Nearly all of the children in the retrospective sample did remember being seen by a psychologist, but only three of the eighteen were able to give any account of what the psychologist's role in the assessment had been. Even in these accounts there were clear indications of confusion about the role of the psychologist. Thus one child reported that 'I had to see him because of my temper tantrums. . . . [He] felt my backbone all the way up and said it was crooked. I don't know why he was doing this.'

The belief that the psychologist 'diagnosed' the cause of children's difficulties came across strongly from these interviews. One child said that during the psychologist's visit he remembered having to play games and reading. According to this boy the purpose of these activities was 'to help him find out what was wrong with me'. Another child said of the assessment: 'That's how I found out I was dyslexic . . . I saw him [the psychologist] because I had learning problems. I saw him and he said I was dyslexic.'

All the children in this sample, retrospectively, complained of a lack of information about the assessment. Parents' beliefs about the assessment could be an additional source of anxiety. One girl, Joanne, reported being told by her mother that the psychologist was a 'brain shrink' which, she said, meant that there must be 'something wrong with your head'.

Few children in the residential school sample were aware of what it meant to have a statement of special educational needs. One child who had heard about statements said that he knew about it 'because my mum got a letter from the psychologist. She thought it meant I was spastic. He told her it meant they could twist a few strings to get me into the RAF which was what I wanted.' Four children thought that a statement was an account of events given to the police. This may not be surprising, but in some cases beliefs about the involvement of the courts may have reflected children's perception of the assessment as a 'punishment'. Thus children reported: 'Our probation officer started it because of what was happening at school'; 'They gave us a choice between a boarding school and a borstal'; and 'The Court and my mum said it would be better for me.'

Very few children whose assessments were directly observed appeared to understand the purpose of those assessments. An exception to this was Stephen, aged 12, whose assessment was taking place whilst he was on an emergency placement in a residential school. Stephen believed the assessment was taking place because 'They need the reports to keep me here because the education are paying and they're going skint.' Like Stephen, where children did have a conception of the purpose of the assessment this tended to be understood in terms of the type of placement it would lead to rather than in terms of how the assessment and subsequent placement might address their educational needs by improving the quality of their schooling. Thus Jason suggested that, although 'I'm not sure what it means. I think it's to see whether I'm capable of going to a mainstream school or not.'

If the purpose of the assessment was unclear to many children, the procedures were a closed book. Yet observations of these assessments revealed strong evidence in support of claims made by psychologists that they had provided children with detailed explanations of what the assessment was about. Perhaps these adults had difficulty in pitching their explanations of these complex bureaucratic procedures at a level which would make sense to the children. On the other hand, it is perhaps not insignificant that this information tended to be provided at the beginning of the assessment, whereas children's anxieties about the assessment were generally greatest towards the latter stages when they became more aware of the likely outcomes. Moreover, it was at this stage that children's suspicions about the real purpose of the assessment, and particularly about the role of the psychologist in that process, became most acute. The lack of trust that many children had for professionals, especially at this stage, made it difficult for the latter effectively to convey information that would be useful to children.

In some cases, the way children were informed that an assessment would be taking place set up their expectations of what would follow. Lee (aged 12) vividly illustrated this point when he commented that the first he heard of the assessment was 'when the letter came. That's the first my mum and dad heard of it as well. I don't know what it's about. My parents don't either.' However, a reference in the LEA's letter to an assessment being initiated under Section 5 of the 1981 Education Act was interpreted by Lee to mean that he was being 'sectioned' under mental health legislation and likely to be placed in a psychiatric hospital; this was a belief that Lee's parents were unwilling or unable to dispel. Although Lee's misperceptions about the assessment process were more extreme than those of many other children in the sample, compounded as they were by a combination of intra-family conflict and LEA insensitivity, they are illustrative of a common problem. In the absence of information children interpreted their experience of the assessment in terms of other experiences in their lives. Thus the assessment could, quite unintentionally, reinforce negative and damaging self-perceptions.

Children's perceptions of the roles of the LEA's professional advisers also suggest how children's expectations of the process may affect interactions occurring between children and professionals. For one 11-year-old visits from the psychologist were a source of bemusement: 'I don't know who he is, but he's a human being. He comes to see me at school. He's never said why he's come to see me.' For John, aged 7, visits from the psychologist were seen to have more sinister implications:

> He's been kind to me but there's something strange about me. I always get to go to see him. Whenever visitors come to school to see children in my class it's always me who has to see them. I don't know why I'm picked out but I think it means there's something odd about me.

Andrew was one of four children who referred to the psychologist as 'a doctor', even if a slightly unusual doctor: 'She's a weirdo who asked me weirdo questions. I think she was a doctor.' Lee expressed an anxiety about seeing a psychologist that was common to many of the children in this sample, when he observed 'My only thought was that I hope he doesn't think there's anything wrong with me.'

Eleven children in the sample expressly identified the psychologist as the key decision-maker affecting their future. Four children explicitly stated that the role of the psychologist was 'to send me away'. For instance, Peter said of his psychologist: 'He wants to send me away. I don't know why. He hasn't told me.' George (aged 9) said that the role of the psychologist was to 'find a place for you to go if you've been bad or you've no home.' By contrast only two children saw the psychologist as someone who would help them to overcome problems in school. One of these, David (aged 13), described his psychologist as someone who 'sorts out problems at school like fighting. A psychiatrist is someone who deals with kids who are backward. A psychologist is someone who deals with kids who have problems.' Interestingly, the source of David's information was not the psychologist but, rather, his older sister.

Children reported that they did not know how psychologists arrived at their recommendations. Angela (aged 14), for instance, knew only that 'He did some tests – maths tests and a daft one, "what goes with 'point', 'blood' and 'water'?" And something about telephone numbers. The tests were to find a school, or at least that's what I guessed they were for.'

Children were even vaguer in their understanding of the contribution of the clinical medical officer to the assessment procedures, other than that this involved a physical check-up. In three cases, however, children interpreted comments made by the doctor during the medical as providing an explanation of the difficulties they were experiencing in school. According to George, who was subsequently placed in a residential school for children with emotional and behavioural difficulties, the clinical medical officer 'told me I kicked with my left foot but write with my right arm and that's what's wrong with me. That's what she said.' The doctor had indeed said something to this effect. Explaining to George and his father what she would say in her report, she listed six observations relating to George's 'medical condition', one of which was: 'That he uses his right eye with his right hand, but left leg. That means that he has a cross-lateral indominance. This could be linked to his specific learning difficulties.' In the other two cases the medical examination was interpreted by children as confirmation of their belief that they were not responsible for their behaviour. After his medical, Graham (aged 9) commented that 'I saw the doctor because I was bad. The doctor told my mum the stuff I wasn't allowed – "E" numbers, colours, additives – things that make you bad. That's what's wrong with me. That's why I'm bad.'

Few children appeared to have discussed the assessment and its possible outcomes with their parents. Lee, for example, stated that 'I don't know what mum and dad want to happen in the future. They don't say much about what I'm doing here [in a residential school on an emergency placement pending the assessment]'. By contrast, five children referred to discussions taking place with their parents, either then or in the future, but prior to any decisions being taken. According to Michael, 'Nobody except my mother has asked me my views about the assessment.' Philip believed that 'Mum decides and she'll ask me what I think.' Terrance's mother had explained to him that 'The assessment will mean I will get extra help in school but I don't know what that will be.' Neither, for that matter, did Terrance's mother. The apparent failure of parents to communicate information about the assessment to their children may reflect their own ignorance and anxieties about that process, yet the significance of tensions and conflicts within families should not be underestimated in this respect.

PERCEPTIONS OF INVOLVEMENT IN DECISION-MAKING

Only two of the seven unit children felt that they had been involved in decisions about their education. In both cases this had been the result of their direct action rather than an outcome of consultation: 'I did a runner [from his mainstream school] because I hated it, because everyone was battering me. I wanted to go to the unit instead of going there.' More typical of the children in this sample was Michael, who commented: 'They didn't tell me about it. I had no ideas of what it would be like.' This sense of powerlessness in relation to the decision-making process was also common amongst children in the residential school sample. These children, without exception, felt their views had not been genuinely sought by anyone in their schools or by any of the other professionals with whom they had been in contact. 'Nobody asked me what I wanted' was a commonly voiced observation. There was an inevitability about the children's resignation to decisions being taken for them by adults. Even where, exceptionally, a child recalled being asked for his views by a psychologist, the report he gave of his response suggested passivity and resignation: 'They asked me but I didn't say owt because I didn't know what to say.'

Not knowing what to say is not quite the same as having nothing to say! The problem for children is not simply that they are provided with no real opportunities to explain their feelings and needs but, more importantly, that they lack the power to create opportunities of their own choosing to address those needs. Buffeted between the assumptions of adult carers and the constraints imposed by the availability of resources Tony (aged 14) painted a despairing yet incisive picture of his feelings of powerlessness. Prior to his current residential school placement he had spent a period of time in a day special school sandwiched between two periods in different mainstream schools:

> I left it [his day special school] because the teachers wanted to try me in a normal school. I went to a school one afternoon a week and was getting on well. I then went full-time to a different school and didn't get on at all. [After that] I used to take a nice walk which was 25 miles round to the special school to see the kids and the teachers. I wish I'd never left there. I would have gone back if I'd had the chance. I would have told them that if they'd asked, but I wouldn't tell them if they didn't because I wanted to be in a normal school.

Tony was quite clear about what he wanted but, none the less, felt unable to express his feelings. Yet he was well aware that this made him the victim of other people's choices. As one of the children in the concurrent sample put it, 'I had no choice really. I'd rather not have a choice.'

Some children did report that they had been asked for their views by their parents but, although they welcomed this opportunity, this could be problematic in its own right, partly because parents often lacked crucial pieces of information but also because conflicts between children and parents made it difficult for the former to 'open up'.

One area of decision-making in respect of which a number of children felt they had been involved concerned the choice over which residential school they should attend. Indeed, some children felt that this decision had been left entirely to them. They were, none the less, aware that the decision was about whether or not to attend a particular residential school, not about the appropriateness of residential schooling itself.

Similar views regarding their own involvement in the decision-making process were expressed by children in the concurrent sample. For the most part, these children believed that no one was interested in their side of the story and that the assessment procedures had not given them an opportunity to express their views. Indeed, there was little evidence of professionals taking systematic steps to identify children's views and take these into account. George's account of his meetings with his educational psychologist is graphic but far from untypical of the experience of other children in the sample:

> I've been visited by someone in school called a socialist [sic]. I didn't like seeing her because I thought they were going to take me away. I couldn't talk to them and tell them about what I felt. They kept talking and I couldn't get a chance to speak. If I had the chance to speak I would have said I didn't want to go away. I wanted to stay with my parents and family.

This does not mean that children never made attempts to influence assessment outcomes. Far from it. Barry confidently saw himself as having the power to make decisions about the outcome of the assessment by means of his refusal to attend any assessment interviews. By absenting himself from school he was no longer seen as a problem by his teachers and the LEA was therefore under little pressure to pursue the assessment with any vigour.

Although the marginalization of children in the 'official' decision-making process was the rule, an exception to this occurred in one case where a child's needs were being jointly assessed by the LEA and the social services department. Mindful of obligations imposed on them by child-care legislation, the social services department took clear steps to ascertain the child's views, using procedures they had established for obtaining and acting upon a 'Personal Statement'. That these procedures actually gave some power to Alistair (aged 16) is evident from the fact that complaints he directed against his social worker resulted in her being taken off his case even though there was no suggestion that she had acted unprofessionally. On the other hand, from Alistair's point of view at least, the voice these procedures gave him was still not sufficient to place him on equal terms with the professionals involved in his case. A change of social worker did not change the decisions that were being made about him. At the end of the day it was he who was being assessed, not the professionals. His vulnerability in the face of the power of these professionals stemmed from that fact:

> No one has listened to my side of events nor to my own wishes. Events at school have been blown out of proportion. My family situation has been over-dramatized. I'm happy at home and I want to stay there. I don't want to be in care and don't deserve to be. I'm upset about the way my mother has been upset and insulted by different professionals. My education has been damaged and I don't know what will happen next. No one has concerned themselves to keep me informed.

CHILDREN'S PERCEPTIONS OF THEIR OWN NEEDS

Perhaps predictably, it tended to be older children who were most concerned about the damage being done to their education rather than younger ones. Even so the primary-aged children attending the unit were still conscious of differences in the educational provision they were now receiving compared to that provided in their mainstream schools. All the unit children commented favourably upon the work they were given to do in the unit, though some were concerned about the lack of opportunities to do PE in particular. The children felt that teachers at the unit were more concerned with helping them and making sure that the level of difficulty of the work was appropriate. One child, however, said that he had found the work harder, because at his mainstream school 'I used to have a teacher on my own for everything.'

For the most part, children at the residential schools were also happier with the work they were now being given and felt that more concern was being shown for their academic needs than previously had been the case. An exception to this was one girl who said that 'I think I'm getting worser. The school is rubbish, absolutely rubbish. I hate being here.' The remaining children reported improvements in the standard of education they were now receiving. These improvements, however, were related to the delivery of the curriculum rather than to its content. In this sense the educational benefits of special schooling were seen by these children as mixed. The lack of breadth to the curriculum offered in the unit and residential schools were identified as a source of frustration, and complaints were made relating to the absence of sports facilities in the unit and the limited number of GCSE options available within the special schools.

A theme arising in many interviews was the isolation that these children had experienced in their mainstream schools as they became trapped in a vicious circle of their own poor behaviour and learning difficulties on the one hand and the neglect or retaliation they believed their teachers had shown towards them on the other. All the children from the two residential schools were insistent that only by leaving their previous schools had they been given a chance to overcome the difficulties they were experiencing. According to John, 'I'm glad I left it. I kept running away because I wanted to leave that school.' Now: 'My behaviour has improved because the teachers are polite, not like at an ordinary school. The teachers at my old school should have been politer and then things would have been better.'

Not all the children were entirely happy that their needs had been met by their placement in the more 'caring' environment of a special school. In two cases acceptance of special schooling was based upon the self-image these children had of themselves as 'problem' children rather than on any preference for the schools in their own right. For these children residential school was seen as a punishment that they deserved. One girl said that she had chosen the first school she had visited, despite disliking it intensely, her reason being that 'I didn't want to put my mum through any more. . . . I put my mum through quite a lot of worry when I was at home . . . [but] I didn't feel very good about having to leave home to come here.' Indeed, almost all the children in this sample didn't want to be away from home and said that they would, if given the choice, have gone back. None the less, with the exceptions noted above, children at both the schools and at the unit felt that, compared with teachers in their mainstream schools, the teachers in these institutions were more understanding and more willing to make genuine efforts to support and encourage them.

Despite having gone through an assessment process resulting in a placement in residential schooling some of these children still resisted the idea that they had 'special needs'. Peter had been told that going to residential school 'was for my own good. [But] I don't know what they mean by that. . . . I've got a record but that's ages ago. I've never got into any really really bad trouble like some of the lads here.' Stuart, by contrast, knew that his assessment had resulted in his being given a 'statement':

It's when you say something about special needs. When you need something. [But] I haven't got special needs. I don't need anything. I don't need any special help. There are a couple of kids here who do need special help. They need help with their school work – reading and things – but I don't.

Stuart's comments were echoed by some of the children in the concurrent sample. Barry, for instance, said that the assessment had been started because 'they said they were going to get me some extra help in school. [But] I haven't got any special needs.' Barry had no idea if this special help had actually been provided for him in school because, since the assessment started: 'I've not been back there.' (Barry would only talk to me when I managed to convince him that I was not from the Educational Welfare Department.)

Only rarely did a child in this sample see the assessment as being related to their own needs. Jason, for whom the statementing process had been initiated to secure resources to support his reintegration into mainstream, did believe that the assessment was concerned with helping him to readjust to his new circumstances. Many more children felt that the assessment was more concerned with the needs of their teachers or parents than their own. Eleven children identified help in resolving conflicts between themselves and/or teachers in school as their most pressing need, whilst three children felt they needed help to sort out problems in their relationships with other family members. A common complaint was that conflicts between pupils in school were resolved arbitrarily without sufficient effort being made to find out what the conflict was about. Sometimes teachers were accused of creating conditions in which conflict between the child and their peers was inevitable. For instance, one boy in the sample reported an occasion when because he had forgotten his PE kit at school his games teacher 'threatened to make me wear a skirt. He called me 'MM' which is short for Mabel Mabbot. It's having a bad influence on me because my mates are all beginning to call me that name.'

Four children did refer to the benefits of there being someone in school to whom they could talk about their problems and who would help in dealing with the conflicts and anxieties of school life. However, where this support was provided as a service within a school it was not always well received. Two children commented on the intrusiveness of school counsellors who 'only want to talk about your family'.

For at least eight children in this sample the assessment was identified as aggravating the difficulties they were experiencing because it reinforced other people's negative images by stigmatizing the child, or because it created conditions in which the child's needs could not be adequately met within their present school. Acceptance by the LEA of a child's formal referral for assessment almost inevitably meant the child would eventually be removed from school. If one considers the number of children (eighteen) who expressed a strong desire to remain in an ordinary school but who were, or expected themselves to be, transferred to a special school as a consequence of the assessment, then the overriding experience these children had of the assessment process was (at least whilst it was in progress) clearly a bad one.

Once her assessment began Angela (correctly) predicted, 'I'll get put away somewhere – sent to a special school for people who are a bit behind. That's how they think of me.' James (aged 15) believed his assessment began 'because they had nowhere else for me to go', but his main concern was that the curriculum at the special school he was to attend was so limited that it might prevent him getting into a career in the RAF: 'The maths scared me a bit because it was the same as I was doing in primary school. I'm worried that I won't be able to do a GCSE in maths.' The assessment was seen by these children as having a logic that had little to do with how they saw their own needs and how they perceived circumstances in their lives (including the assessment itself) to have created these or prevented them from being met.

The length of time taken to complete the assessment procedures was also seen as a source of new difficulties for some children. James's assessment began after his permanent exclusion from school in November 1989, 'pending psychological advice'. However, a final statement was not issued until January 1991 and a school place did not materialize until the following Easter, which meant that his final GCSE year had to be retaken. Alistair's experience was similar, once he had been excluded from his academically prestigious grammar school. As various agencies spent more than a year trying to decide whether or not he should be placed in special education he complained, 'My education has been damaged and I don't know what will happen next.'

Angela had a similar experience. Over a two- or three-year period before her permanent exclusion from school she had experienced the traumatic upheavals of her mother's death, her rejection by foster parents on two occasions and her own attempted suicide. Her exclusion from school and the subsequent reluctance of other local head teachers to take her in led the LEA to believe that they could only offer a residential school placement even though this would entail her leaving the children's home in which she had expressed a strong desire to remain. Although she was 14 years old she was not involved in these deliberations. Compared to the DFE's recommended time-scale for completion of assessments under the 1981 Act Angela received priority treatment but this did nothing to ease her anxieties: 'I'm definitely bothered about what's going to happen. It's dragged on for a long time – too long. It's been four months and I get fed up.'

THE CHILD'S PERCEPTION OF THE EFFECTS OF THE ASSESSMENT UPON STATUS IN SCHOOL, THE FAMILY AND PEER GROUP

In one-off interviews with children it is difficult to build up the trust which would allow family and peer-group relationships to be examined in detail. Naturally some children were defensive and reluctant to discuss these sensitive issues. Furthermore, in this area more than any other, it is difficult to assess whether children are giving genuine expression to their feelings or merely saying how they would like things to be in an ideal world. This was, of course, an issue of concern in analysing all the retrospective interviews. In respect of these interviews it is only possible to report what the children said, always bearing in mind the caution that has been expressed.

In fact, no children in the unit sample acknowledged their placement to have had an effect on their status in the family. Their main concerns were, rather, those of establishing their status in the unit itself and managing their relationships with their peers outside the unit. Six of the seven children in the sample talked of their anxieties on first going to the unit and the importance of establishing themselves in a 'tough' environment. Paul recalled with horror that 'I thought the other children would be really dangerous and come with penknives.' Matthew had been told by his teacher in mainstream school that the unit 'was nice' but he took more seriously the warnings of a friend who had already been to the unit: 'He told me it was horrible.' Anxieties about how 'rough' the children in the unit must be made it important for the children in this sample to establish themselves as equally 'tough' or 'tougher' from the beginning. As Matthew put it: 'When I first came they were rough with me but now none dare.' One of the children in the residential schools sample described a similar experience which occurred when he was attending a unit similar to the one in this study. He recalled that, whilst at the unit, he had to travel each day from the other side of town: 'I got picked on rotten by other boys at the unit. They picked on me because of where I came from. They said "You don't pay your poll tax" and all that lot. I didn't like it so I hit some and they hit me back.'

For five of the children an even greater concern had been the effects of their placement on their relationships with friends in their neighbourhoods and in the mainstream schools they had, at various times, continued to attend for part of each week. Three strategies were employed to deal with the difficulties they encountered. Craig and Liam avoided any mention of the unit. Liam said that friends at his mainstream school had asked him about it but: 'I said nothing. I didn't want them to know.' Craig's friends in his mainstream school 'think I stay well away from school. They don't ask so I don't tell them.' This latter comment, though essentially conveying avoidance of the issue, also contains a hint of a second strategy; namely, that of ascribing a higher status to what is done when not attending mainstream school.

This was the strategy adopted by Martin when the way he was treated in school by his teachers made it very obvious that he was special. On the half day of each week when he attended his mainstream primary school as part of a reintegration programme: 'I wasn't taught in a classroom. I had to sit outside the headmaster's office and the headmaster's secretary's secretary [*sic*] gave me work. I wasn't allowed out to play.' Later in the year, 'I went in a classroom, the one below mine! in age. I didn't do the same kind of work as the other kids. I did puzzles. They did maths and things.' Perhaps not surprisingly, 'Other children in my primary school ask a lot of questions. "Is it good?" I said, "Yes, it's better than here." They wanted to come here.'

Two children in the unit sample had been the focus of unwelcome attention from their peers because of their attendance at the unit. Paul said that children in his neighbourhood 'keep asking me all questions about the school. By the time they've finished I feel fed up. Everyone goes "Which school do you go to?" and I really hate that.' Matthew was upset because 'some people call me "Sherburn" round our way – that's a school for disabled people'. In response to taunts these children went on the offensive. Paul teased them back 'for going to a really strict school', whilst Matthew 'hit them if I get them'.

The experiences of children attending the residential schools were not as pronounced in this respect as those of the children in the unit. This, no doubt, reflected the fact that the former did not have to deal with their neighbourhood peers on a day-to-day basis. Three children maintained that their status amongst peers at home had improved since going away to school. No mention of any major problems with neighbourhood peer groups was made by the remainder. One girl said that, since coming to this school, she had lost contact with friends at home. Another child who made a similar comment about some of her friends at home did so more positively, believing that it was her association with them that had got her into trouble in the first place.

Concerns about the effect of a placement in residential school on their status within their families was similarly not strongly expressed by children in this sample. Not surprisingly some children were upset by the deterioration in family relationships prior to their placement, but only two out of the eleven voiced any unease about their position in the family as a direct consequence of being placed in the school. For one of these, the placement was seen as providing his family with a way of getting rid of him: 'I don't think I'm allowed home any more. I don't think my parents like me any more.' By contrast, two children, both girls, were very positive about what they saw as the beneficial consequences of their placement in a residential school for their relationships with other members of their families. Rachel said that now:

> When I go home I don't argue as much with my mum. . . . When I was at my other school I used to argue with her all the time. Now when I go home dad takes me out in the car with my little brother. I get on a lot better with my family since I've been here.

Bernadette said that, since going away to school, 'My parents are liking me more because my behaviour is getting better. I can help my mum more and get on with people better.'

The experiences of Rachel and Bernadette suggest support for the findings of a recent study of pupils' perceptions of residential schooling. In a study of two schools for children with emotional and behavioural difficulties (Cooper 1989) found that respite from problems located in the home situation can lead to positive outcomes, including improvements in the pupils' self-images. He argued that simply by breaking the cycle of involvement in distressing circumstances at home and in school, by relief from the circumstances which maintain their problems, children may be empowered to confront those difficulties in ways that enhance rather than undermine their self-image.

Fear about the outcome of the assessment and its consequences was common amongst those children who were currently going through the process. These fears were sometimes expressed in graphically lurid ways. Thus, Graham was sure that in residential schools 'they batter you with canes', whilst Peter declared that he didn't want to be sent there because 'boys are put in straitjackets when they're naughty'. Yet for Graham, at least, the prospect of having to endure such a regime gave him kudos with his mainstream peers: 'It showed the other children I was tough.' For Michael also, his exclusion from school and subsequent placement in a residential school led in his eyes to an increase in his status amongst neighbourhood friends: 'Because I've been expelled my friends just wind me up because I'm a good lad.' For six of the children the assessment confirmed their belief either that they were ill or that they were in some other way unable to control their own behaviour. Gavin, for instance, was resigned to the fact that 'I think it's something in me. I don't think I'll ever be good.'

No one directly involved in Philip's assessment suggested to him that he had a food allergy but none the less the fact that the assessment was taking place, in his view, provided confirmation of his inability to control his temper, which he put down to 'what I eat – things like cornflakes, coke and bread'. One child believed that the continuous flow of visitors he received during his assessment meant that there must be something 'odd' about him. For other children the assessment led to their becoming resigned to the labels placed on them by their teachers and other adults. After being told that he was to be sent to a residential school, George (aged 9) made the following observation on his plight:

> I was naughty a lot at school. People came to see me a lot because I was naughty. Lots of people. I thought it was not good for me to be bad but I couldn't help being bad. . . . My parents and all the other people thought I was bad. They wanted to send me to a children's home because I was being bad. I was sad. They thought it would stop making me bad. I thought it wouldn't but I wanted to be good.

When Nick's parents removed him from an off-site unit and, with the support of a sympathetic head teacher, placed him in a new mainstream school, effectively putting an end to the formal assessment that had been in progress, Nick (aged 8) stated that 'now I'm not going to be naughty because I'm not going to the unit. They said I don't have to go to the unit any more. Then I can start being good.' When he was attending the unit he acknowledged that he had been naughty because 'everyone was nasty to me so I was nasty to them.' In Nick's eyes his attendance at the unit meant that he had to be bad *because he was bad*. Whereas the assessment appeared to be confirming that 'badness', once he left the unit and the assessment was abandoned he was freed from the need to be bad. The success of his reintegration into this mainstream primary over the following months would seem to support this interpretation.

Anxieties about the implications of the assessment for their place within their families was another major area of concern, especially for those children who expected to be placed in residential schools. Lee was convinced that 'There's people in the class a lot worse than me – so why do I have to go into a home?' As far as he could see, the only reason was that his mother wanted him out of the family.

> Personally I can't see anything wrong with me. Mum thinks there's something wrong with me. Mum is the only one in the house who's suggesting it. . . . It makes me feel bad towards my mum. I wonder what she's doing this for.

Lee's mother did think there was 'something wrong in his head', and it was she who had pressed for the assessment to be initiated, against the wishes of Lee's father and despite assurances from the school that they did not find Lee's behaviour unmanageable. This was one of a number of cases in which the assessment was manipulated by family members who were in conflict with one another over issues not necessarily related to the needs of the child. This was a recurring theme in the study, as participants in the assessment, including teachers as well as family members, negotiated and manipulated the needs of children who were being assessed to match conceptions of their own needs.

George said that since his assessment had started he had been upset because his older brother had kept saying, 'I want you to go', and his younger brother had also told him to 'go' and 'I want you to die.' Most of all he had been upset by 'mum and dad wanting me to go'. . . . I don't know why they want me to go.' The irony of this was that George's parents had throughout resisted the recommendations of the professionals for George to be placed in a residential school, only conceding when they felt they were no longer being given any real choice. Yet George's misperceptions, if that was what they were, of what his family wanted were powerfully reinforced by the assessment process.

Other children felt that their relationships with family members had deteriorated, in consequence of the assessment outcome, because they were no longer seen as part of the family. In these circumstances, visits home at weekends or in the holidays could prove traumatic. Michael, for instance, found that 'My sisters have changed since I've been here [residential school]. I fell out with my sisters in the holidays and my dad hit me in the face. I nutted him. I got a knife and was put in the cells.'

None of the children in this sample felt that their relationships with other family members had been improved by the assessment/placement, and in this respect the experiences of this group may be contrasted with the two children in the retrospective sample who spoke in positive terms about this effect of the assessment.

Peer-group relationships were seen as important by all the children in this sample. Some children were concerned about how the assessment might affect their relationships with peers. However, it was not being labelled 'violent' or 'disruptive' that was the cause of this concern but, rather, any suggestion that they might be 'remedial' or 'backward'. After his admission to a school for children with emotional and behavioural difficulties James was taken aback by the reaction of former friends whom he had known in his mainstream school: 'Everyone seems to be "taking the Michael" about the school I'm going to being a remedial centre. . . . They think it's a school for "mental" kids.'

There was also evidence that children felt themselves to be increasingly marginalized in their schools because of the assessment that was taking place, and this did not help to resolve the conflicts that already existed with other pupils. Indeed, it seems that other children might have been actively dissuaded by teachers from playing with children who had been referred for assessment. In other cases the mere fact of being excluded from school meant that children were denied the normal contact with their peers that occurs as a part of school life. This was often so for very long periods.

CONCLUSION

Neglect and disregard of children's own views about their present experiences and future needs has a long history and, despite recent attempts to empower children with a voice in matters that affect them (most notably in the 1989 Children Act but also, in a more modest way, in the 1993 Education Act), old habits die hard. Despite these legislative initiatives, involving children in decision-making demands much more than rhetoric backed up with good intentions. This chapter has looked at the experience of children who have been the subject of special educational needs assessments. These children commonly alluded to their experience of assessment as removing any control they might previously have had over events and over public understanding of those events. Almost invariably this disempowerment reflected the decisions of professionals about how the 'problem' should (or in practice must) be conceptualized. Children of all ages were frequently found to be confused about the purpose of their assessments and about the roles of adult participants. Children did not believe they had been given an opportunity to tell their side of the story. There was generally a recognition on their part that they had been experiencing difficulties at school and/or at home and that they needed help to overcome these, but only rarely did a child see the assessment as providing a meaningful framework within which the various dimensions of these difficulties could be explored and worked out. From the perspective of many children, if the assessment was concerned with anybody's needs it was concerned with the needs of their teachers and parents. These children had a strong sense that the outcome would not, and could not, be influenced by their own wishes. This belief was not necessarily well-founded because there were indications from various professionals that they would have welcomed the child's point of view if this had been forthcoming, yet, surprisingly, there was little evidence to indicate that the professionals concerned had made any serious attempts to gain access to the children's views. Anxieties about the assessment were common-place and, in the rather less threatening context of a research interview, children did give voice to their concerns about how the assessment might, or already did, affect their futures. In particular, many children believed that the assessment isolated them and made them stand out as different.

A sharp contrast can be seen between the views of professionals, who emphasized that the child was their principal client whose interests should be served by the assessment, and the lack of attention apparently given to the child's voice in those assessments. One could argue that this was because children had little to say, but the accounts described in this chapter appear to suggest otherwise. Alternatively, it might be argued that profes-sionals are often inadequately trained in the use of techniques for gaining access to the child's perspective. There is probably some truth in this but it is unlikely to be the whole story. As we shall see, there are other pressures which work against attempts by professionals to involve chil-dren in decision-making, pressures which promote the child as the 'victim' of intellectual, emotional or social disadvantages in need of specialist professional help.

Chapter 6

The child's contribution to the assessment
The negotiation of deviant identities

In Chapters 1–3 it was argued that parent–professional interactions during assessments of children's special educational needs take place within a wider social context of competing and frequently conflicting interests. Professionals, including teachers, doctors, psychologists, and members of other caring and administrative professions, cannot simply take on a neutral role; they have their own professional interests in the assessment process and its outcomes. They are also engaged in negotiations with both parents and other professionals about ownership of clients, service strategies and resource priorities: negotiations which give meaning to the way in which the 'needs' of all participants in an assessment come to be understood. In these negotiations the power of participants to influence how and what consensus is reached in the assessment is not equally distributed. In consequence, the scope parents have, within the official procedures, for achieving outcomes not supported by, or in opposition to, professionals will be limited.

Children may be bound by constraints similar to those operating on their parents, and this is so despite recent attempts to give children a voice in decision-making about their special educational needs (DES 1989a; DFE 1994). In Chapter 5 evidence was reviewed which suggested that children's experiences of the assessment process are often ones of bewilderment and confusion. A case can clearly be made for providing more information as well as better-quality information for children. However, in this chapter it will be argued that there are forms of control implicit in the assessment system and that these forms of control operate to reproduce the power of professionals over their clients.

The assessment of special educational needs by professionals, together with the 'objective measures' used to identify children's needs, can be understood at different levels, each of which may be seen as authentic but which, none the less, have contradictory implications. There is no reason to believe that professionals act in anything other than good faith. Professionals generally recognize the child as their principal client and understand their own role in terms of identifying the child's needs and then representing her or his interests. Interviews with children are crucial to this process; thus, it can be argued that by gaining access to the child's views the improved quality of information available to professionals will lead to improvements in the quality of decision-making in respect of that child's education. Yet, professionals' interviews with children are also social events in which meanings and perspectives are negotiated. Once again, both the professional and the child may act in good faith in these negotiations, but seen at this level the interview is a decision-making event rather than simply an information-gathering exercise.

In this chapter it will be argued that, despite recent advances in thinking about the nature of interactions taking place between professionals and children, and how these interactions might affect children's contributions within interview situations (see Chapter 4), there is still little evidence of professionals incorporating this thinking into their practice in special education assessments. It is unlikely to be the case that professionals intentionally disempower children. None the less, research does suggest that consideration is rarely given by professionals to the way in which power embedded in their own roles may result in children being disempowered. Disempowerment occurs where the assessment process not only denies the child a voice but where it also denies that child the opportunity to develop and represent alternative frameworks for understanding the origin and construction of the needs of all participants.

THE MEDICAL ASSESSMENT

The medical examination forms part of the statutory procedures of an assessment under the 1981 Education Act. However, the Act stipulates no requirements regarding the format of the medical assessment, nor the nature of the information to be reported upon. Twelve medical examinations were observed in the course of my own research on special needs assessments. These medical interviews invariably took place at the doctor's clinic and in each case the child was accompanied by a parent, guardian or social worker. Children were physically examined, usually following district health authority guidelines, which incorporated a checklist.

Interviews with clinical medical officers (CMOs) revealed that they were generally unclear about their role in respect of assessments under the 1981 Act, especially where learning and/or behavioural difficulties were a significant feature of the case. Some CMOs explained that they were reluctant to provide detailed accounts of children's needs to the LEA because they lacked confidence in their own professional expertise in a non-medical area, and consequently doctors generally saw their contribution to the assessment purely in terms of screening for possible physical, neurological and psychiatric factors which, up to that time, had escaped recognition.

Clinical medical officers are rarely in a position to have close contact over a sustained period of time with a child who is being assessed. Perhaps in consequence of this the CMOs in the study felt very reliant on the reports of professional colleagues in the schools and the schools' psychological service. Although they recognized that their lack of close contact with the child imposed constraints on the quality of insight into a child's difficulties which their assessment could provide, when interviewed CMOs frequently expressed strong opinions about the origins and nature of children's difficulties. Thus, prior to one child's medical interview, and before any personal contact had been established with that child, a doctor commented to the researcher that George 'showed very disturbed behaviour, picking on other children and bad language'.

It would be a fine line that would have to be drawn between the desirability of professionals having access to detailed information on the child from other professional colleagues and the preservation in each case of independent professional judgement. Yet, in this study, there was little evidence of any safeguards operating, either at the level of local authority policy or individual practice, to provide professionals with a framework for the assessment which would ensure the independence of their contribution. In the absence of appropriate guidelines the opinions professionals have about the origins of children's difficulties may have a significant but unwarranted impact on the final outcome of the assessment procedure. Additionally, through their interpersonal interaction with children during the assessment, professionals also contribute in significant ways to how children and their parents understand children's difficulties.

Doctors in the study were rarely shy about expressing the personal values upon which their professional judgements were built. One doctor graphically expressed a theme that arose in a number of interviews with CMOs: 'The professionals are standing up for the norms of society, the unwritten rules of the heart. These are akin to boundaries you do not cross – hitting, biting, spitting – things that save the culture.' Particular emphasis was laid by CMOs upon factors in children's home backgrounds. One doctor, for instance, when questioned about a child's difficulties, referred to parents who were 'inadequate'. According to another CMO, the problems experienced by a child he was assessing probably came about because 'he wasn't disciplined enough when he was younger'. It is perhaps not surprising that doctors tended to invoke a medical model of special educational needs. One, for instance, described a child's difficulties in terms of an 'illness' that needed to be 'treated'. However, it was interesting that this concept of illness was also frequently extended beyond the child to include the whole family: 'Families need therapy, not just children. It's no good curing a child if they are simply returned to the same environment.'

By contrast, the difficulties that children experienced in schools were rarely referred to by CMOs, but where this occurred it was invariably in terms of the failure of the child to adjust to his or her school. There was no evidence of any attempt on the part of CMOs to consider the child's behavioural or learning difficulties in the context of school organization, curriculum or interpersonal relationships.

THE PSYCHOLOGICAL ASSESSMENT

Following the recommendations of the Warnock Report (DES 1978), psychologists in many local authorities now have responsibility for co-ordinating the work of all professionals involved in assessments of special educational needs (Goacher et al. 1988). This responsibility may invest psychologists with the power to make recommendations leading to the initiation of an assessment, the collation of reports, and even, as in one of the authorities in this study, the preparation for the LEA of a preliminary draft of the statement of special educational needs. The central role of the educational psychologist in the assessment process could provide her or him with information which would allow a more holistic picture of the child's needs than that available to other professionals, including the child's teachers.

The resources of the schools' psychological services in each of the three LEAs participating in the study were clearly stretched, and there were long waiting lists for children to be seen. Once formal assessments began, however, they were generally completed within a twelve-month period. Although the time taken in almost all the assessments exceeded the DFE's (1994) recommendations that they should be completed within six months, the time taken to carry out these assessments does appear to compare favourably with the general picture reported by the Audit Commission (1992). It might have been the case that the assessments were speeded up because those involved were aware that they were being monitored by a researcher. On the other hand, at least fifteen of the children in the sample had been referred by their teachers as 'urgent cases' and psychologists were clearly under pressure from teachers to prioritize these cases.

The work of educational psychologists is not confined to formal assessments under the 1981 Act, although the psychologists in this study commonly complained that this work took up a far greater proportion of their time than they would have liked. Psychologists reported that children are often seen on a number of occasions before a decision to initiate the formal assessment procedures is taken, and if this is so then it suggests evidence of Warnock's three informal stages of assessment being followed. However, in sixteen of the twenty-nine cases in this study psychologists made their recommendation to commence formal procedures immediately following an initial interview with the child and/or parents, whilst thirteen children were seen on more than one occasion before to this decision was taken. Evidence of sustained involvement with a child on the part of a psychologist (e.g. the child being seen on two or more occasions in different contexts, followed by a written report to the child's teachers making recommendations in respect of behaviour management techniques, curriculum advice, advice on classroom organization, obtaining classroom support and so on) was found in no more than four cases. This is indicative of the gap, in these authorities at least, which existed between practice at the time of the research (1989–91), more than ten years after the Warnock Report's recommendations, and the current expectations of the DFE (1994). Attention has already been drawn to how the expectations of teachers when making their initial referral to the schools' psychological service affect the subsequent decision-making of other professionals involved in these assessment procedures. In twenty-one of the twenty-nine cases the initial referral of children to the schools' psychological service by their teachers was accompanied by a request for a formal assessment under the provisions of the 1981 Education Act.

With only one exception, each of the children was interviewed by an educational psychologist at some stage during the assessment. The exception was a teenager who had gone missing from home, and in this case the psychologist relied upon a report prepared by a colleague who had worked with the child in his primary school. Teachers and parents were also interviewed in every case. However, only five children were observed in the classroom. In most cases psychologists appeared willing to accept teachers' accounts of children's classroom behaviour without recourse to independent observation. This finding was surprising and may well have been unrepresentative, although it does suggest the need for a more detailed study of practice in this area. Equally surprising was the finding that in twelve of the twenty-nine cases in this study psychologists did not regard a home visit as a necessary part of their assessment. This probably reflected the considerable demands which are placed on psychologists' time. It was worrying, however, that in four of the thirteen cases in which psychologists recommended placements in residential special schools after home circumstances had been identified as the principal cause of children's difficulties, home visits had not been made. One psychologist explained her reluctance to visit one of these children at home as follows: 'I very much go on reports people tell me. It's not possible to do everything. I feel I'm the only person who is going to look at that child in terms of ability.' Another psychologist complained of the lack of information available about a child's home situation but none the less still maintained that it was not her job to visit the family herself:

> Ideally we should have known more about George and his family. Of all the agencies we approached we didn't receive any information. That's why I would like a social work assessment. A child shouldn't go off to residential school without a social work assessment [but] the case was in crisis and I was heavily pressured and home visits do take up a lot of time.

In their written reports, psychologists placed heavy reliance upon the results of psychometric testing and upon second-hand information from teachers and parents. By contrast, hardly any psychologists referred to children's strengths within the home and school and in only three cases was there any serious attempt to report the child's perception of his or her difficulties in school and/or home. This was despite the invariable acknowledgement by psychologists that the child was their principal client. In practice, the apparent emphasis upon psychometric testing served little purpose other than to provide some form of legitimacy for the involvement of psychological experts in the assessment. This was particularly the case with intelligence testing, which appeared to be used more because it is widely recognized as part of a psychologist's repertoire of specialist skills than because of any information added by such testing to an understanding of children's needs. Indeed, despite the common use of psychometric testing, psychologists rarely expressed any confidence in these measures as tools for identifying children's needs.

SOURCES OF EMPOWERMENT AND DISEMPOWERMENT FOR CHILDREN WITHIN THE ASSESSMENT

In Chapter 5 it was shown how children's accounts of their own needs tended to accept a personal deficit model of needs. Thus, children might acknowledge that they had difficulty in controlling their behaviour but in doing so they were reluctant to accept responsibility for this, although accounts of causality varied. Some children cited psychological causes – for instance, that they had an uncontrollable temper or that they were 'psycho' – others attributed their difficulties to quasi-medical causes such as 'dyslexia', or to aspects of their environments – for example, what they ate. In constructing these accounts children were heavily influenced by their parents and teachers as well as by the professionals who became involved only at the formal stages of the assessment. Lee, who believed that he was to be committed to a psychiatric hospital after being told that he was to be assessed under Section 5 of the 1981 Education Act was clearly influenced by his mother, whose belief that he was suffering from a psychiatric disorder led her to interpret the LEA's letter initiating the assessment in this way. Teachers and parents both frequently commented on the deterioration in children's behaviour once an assessment had started and, although this could reflect a belief held by children that everyone had given up on them so why should they bother, there was evidence in at least four cases that children believed that the decision to start an assessment had been made because of their intrinsic personality defects. The process by which children internalized the labels constructed through the assessment, however, was not straightforward.

Research reported in Houghton *et al.* (1988) and in Wheldall and Merrett (1988) indicated that the classroom behaviours most commonly identified by teachers as troublesome were those which caused recurrent disruption to the smooth management of learning. Accounts given by teachers participating in my own research identified troublesome behaviours primarily in terms of their disturbing effects on others (colleagues and other children). In so far as behaviour is identified as disturbing in the context of interactions occurring between the child and others, the child may be seen as a participant in the negotiation of her or his own reality. The process of assessment, however, changes the child from agent to 'victim' – a victim of an emotional disturbance, a victim of family pathology and, it could be argued, even a victim of a school's inability to cope. The disempowerment of the child in matters affecting their future is implicit in this victimization, not only because it legitimates the imposition of controls but also because it constructs the child's identity in ways which deny legitimacy to the child's perspective. If, as is widely maintained (for example, Galloway and Goodwin 1987), the concept of emotional and behavioural difficulties is clinically meaningless, then it is reasonable to ask what function the label actually serves. Despite the explicit focus on the child, special needs assessments are more generally concerned with negotiations about the 'needs' of those who are disturbed by the child's behaviour. In this way the label 'emotional and behavioural difficulties' serves to legitimate the needs of others, including teachers, families and peers. Therefore, any attempt to include the child in the decision-making process is premised upon the validity of the label and as such is likely to have disempowering consequences for the child. An unintended consequence of the LEA's decision to initiate an assessment might be that of undermining the validity of the child's perspective, subordinating it to the interpretation of needs assumed by those, usually teachers but sometimes parents, requesting the assessment.

THE ROLE OF THE ASSESSMENT IN INTRA-FAMILY CONFLICT

The procedures for formally assessing children with special educational needs can easily become a focal point for intra-family conflicts. Disputes between children and their parents and/or siblings were a significant feature in the assessment of children participating in my research. The attachment of labels to children, such as 'special educational needs', 'emotional and behavioural difficulties', 'disabled', 'specific learning difficulties' and so on, may satisfy parental 'needs' for an explanation of the difficulties experienced by their children and may also be understood by parents as absolving them from blame or responsibility for their children's problems. However, children may also set their own agendas for the assessment in an attempt to negotiate their status within the family and the wider community.

The behaviour of children may at times be motivated, as Gavin's appeared to be, by the need to 'test' whether they are really loved unconditionally by their parents. For other children, as with Sean, the assessment leading to a placement in a residential special school might be seen as providing a way out of an intolerable family situation without being made to feel responsible for the disintegration of their families which might follow if they were taken into care.

Bryan's mother was anxious for him to be assessed because she believed he was suffering from a psychiatric disorder, but for Bryan his assessment provided an opportunity to challenge that identity and to draw

attention to inconsistencies between his mother and father in their treatment of him. Although he did not admit to this, it seems likely that he was
manipulating the psychologist into supporting his father against his
mother. After one interview with the psychologist Bryan reported with
satisfaction that 'It was obvious nothing was wrong'.

Peter complained bitterly throughout his assessment about the way his
older brother tried to turn other members of his family against him: 'I get
picked on by John. He's picked on me since I saw the psychiatrist when
I was 6. He thinks I don't fit into the family. He calls me "spaz" and
"mental".' The decision to initiate an assessment of his special needs was
seen by Peter as giving credibility to this view, and his parents' eventual
support for the decision to place him in a residential special school left
him feeling rejected by his family.

George said that after his assessment had begun he had been upset
because his older brother had kept saying 'I want you to go' and his
younger brother had told him to 'go' and 'I want you to die.' Most of all
he had been upset by 'mum and dad wanting me to go. . . . I don't know
why they want me to go.' The irony was that George's parents had
throughout resisted the recommendations made by professionals that
George be placed in a residential school, only conceding when they felt
that they were no longer being given any real choice. Yet the assessment
had isolated him within his family and his misperceptions of what his
parents wanted were powerfully reinforced by the outcome of that process.

THE PROFESSIONAL INTERVIEW AS A SOURCE OF CHILDREN'S DISEMPOWERMENT

In Chapter 4 attention was drawn to the difficulties professionals have to
take account of in their attempts to gain access to the child's perspective.
In Chapter 3 it was also argued that factors appertaining to the role of
professionals in the assessment process can create barriers between professionals and parents which impede the former in their attempt to gain
access to parents' views. Similar impediments may also affect communication between children and professionals with significant consequences
for the child's ability to negotiate (what is from her or his point of view)
a satisfactory outcome.

Dr Thomas saw George who was aged 9 towards the end of an
assessment which had lasted for over twelve months. She was aware that
'his parents [had] failed to keep appointments' on two previous occasions
when George ought to have attended for the statutory medical examination. When interviewed by the researcher immediately before the medical

took place, Dr Thomas indicated that there was some medical 'evidence of George having epilepsy and there has been a history of convulsions when he was quite young.' The report on George, which she had received from the educational psychologist in the case, indicated that George had 'a behaviour problem' as well as 'a specific learning difficulty'. Dr Thomas was also aware from the reports that 'George has been admitted to a weekly boarding school for maladjusted children but he doesn't want to go back to boarding school [after spending the weekend at home] on Monday mornings.' In fact, either the information contained in the report was incorrect or the doctor had misunderstood the reports she had been sent. George was not, and had never, attended a special school of any kind. The information probably referred to George's younger brother who was attending a weekly boarding school for children with moderate learning difficulties.

The CMO opened her interview with George by stating that it was taking place because of 'this statementing process: " 'I have to send a report to the education department and the education department will decide which school George will go to." ' Thus, a clear indication was given by the doctor that the purpose of the medical assessment was related to a decision about school placement rather than to an assessment of George's needs. The subtlety of this distinction was not lost on George, who afterwards identified this interview with the CMO as the point at which he realized that the assessment really would result in his placement in a residential school. This was also to have consequences for George's behaviour. Shortly after the medical his mother reported that 'He's still a handful, but now he's very upset now he knows. He's been for a medical and he's very upset. Since his medical he's been crying every morning.'

The structure of the interview and the lines of questioning pursued were indicative of the CMO's perspective on the probable causes of the disturbing behaviour presented by George rather than any attempt to examine all the parameters that might be involved. Thus, George and his father were questioned about 'social problems in the family', about George's relationships with his brothers and sisters, about his relationship with his grandparents, about his attitude towards girls, about his sexual development, about his eating habits, his sleeping habits, his television viewing, about his behaviour and temper at home, about the smoking habits of family members, and about psychiatric problems in the family. Throughout this interview the doctor asked only two questions relating to George's school – 'Is there anybody at school who you don't like?' – to which George replied, 'Those who are picking on me'; and, 'Do you like to play with girls at school?' to which George replied 'No'. The first question was not followed up by the CMO whilst the second was followed up by a question about his testicles. The general line of inquiry was pursued quite exclusively by the CMO, despite being told by George's father that 'Everything he does is the same as any normal child does. It's just this crying and his behaviour at school and swearing at teachers.'

At one point in the interview Dr Thomas asked George: 'Who would you like to take to the moon with you if you were going? Your mum, your dad, your brother or your sister?' After some hesitation George replied that he would take his dad. The significance of this question was not immediately apparent. When subsequently interviewed Dr Thomas explained that its purpose was to reveal the child's thinking about his family: 'George doesn't like his mother. That's unusual. He chose to take his father to the moon and not his mother. It looks like it's a childhood depression.' At one level this is an absurd statement, a case perhaps of 'a little knowledge being a dangerous thing'. This might be considered particularly insidious because no opportunity was given to George or his parents to contest the CMO's interpretation. On the other hand, because the CMO's views were not revealed to George or his parents, it could be argued that they would not have any direct effect on his self-concept. Yet, it is not insignificant in terms of the construction of his future identity as a 'disturbed' child. This interview was not concerned simply with identifying George's needs; it also involved a negotiation *about* the problem. The lack of control the child was able to exert over the content of the interview contributed to George's continuing disempowerment in the assessment process. What is significant about the CMO's questioning in this interview is that it was she who was setting the context within which the meaning of George's difficulties at school were being understood – that is, as a depressive condition caused by family problems. This understanding was subsequently used by her to support the consensus reached amongst all the professionals involved about George's disturbing *classroom* behaviour. As it was defined as a family problem, the school context in which George's disturbing behaviour had occurred was treated as unproblematic and therefore unexplored. This 'consensus' entailed a very explicit construction of George's deviant identity (unmanageable at school and uncontrolled at home) with profound consequences for his future (placement in a residential special school).

The way power is defined by professionals in their interactions with children during assessment events suggests how children may be denied a voice in these procedures. In this study, where the assessment was seen by children to be in response to teachers' or parents' perception of the 'problem' it was often seen by them as part of their punishment. Nineteen of the twenty-nine children in this sample explicitly referred to the assessment in these terms. Thus the assessment could be seen by children as an expression of the power their schools and/or parents had to determine their 'reality' rather than as offering a framework within which *they* could contribute to the definition of the 'problem'. Genuine empowerment of the child within the formal procedures of the assessment may only be possible, therefore, where that assessment focuses upon the full range of interactions affecting that child, including those in which she or he is not directly involved (such as policy decisions, funding decisions and so on), as well as those in which the child is a participant. Where this is not the case the child's involvement can only serve to promote what Goffman (1968) referred to as a 'spoiled identity'. Saying nothing might be a symptom of the child's disempowerment induced by the assessment itself rather than merely a consequence of inadequate opportunities being provided by professionals for children to express their needs. One of the children in the sample, Michael, put it like this: 'I didn't want to be away from my family and friends. . . [but] there was nothing I could say really because they wouldn't have me back in school.'

For another child, however, saying nothing manifested itself in a deliberate strategy of absenting himself from both assessment interviews and school. Once Barry was 'out of their hair' his assessment was no longer a priority for his teachers and other professionals. Barry's head of year argued that Barry's absence from school meant that he could now 'redirect my attention to those with whom I'm likely to get the biggest results. . . . If you talk to the staff here, their first reaction will be relief that he's not attending.'

Despite the reluctance of many children to contribute their views to the assessment there was evidence of children seeking to influence the outcome of their assessments and also, in some situations, of professionals embracing the child's perspective in so far as it supported those professions in pursuit of their own agendas.

EMPOWERMENT AND INTER-PROFESSIONAL CONFLICT

Carl, although only 7 at the time of his assessment, was exceptional amongst the children in this sample in that his views were taken seriously. Yet this case was also exceptional in that from the beginning there was a broad consensus amongst parents, class teacher, head teacher and educational psychologist. After some preliminary work with Carl by the psychologist the LEA agreed to appoint a classroom assistant to help with his management in the classroom. This classroom assistant was employed by the LEA's support services and not by the school. Conflict between the classroom assistant and the class teacher and head teacher of the school over the role the former was to have in the classroom revolved around Carl's deteriorating behaviour. Concern expressed by Carl's mother about this situation led to a joint request for the psychologist to carry out a formal assessment, which it was hoped would lead to specific recommendations for Carl's management supported by the legal status of a statement of special educational needs. This was a strategy which was supported by the psychologist, and an 'alliance' was formed between head teacher, parent and psychologist directed towards bringing the classroom assistant under the control of the school. The shared agenda of these adults led to considerable emphasis being placed on Carl's view of his deteriorating relationships with other children in his class and how this was affecting his behaviour at home. Thus Carl was empowered by key professionals involved in his assessment because his perspective supported and legitimated their own recommendations.

Although Carl's assessment was characterized by a broad consensus amongst professionals and between professionals and parents, in other cases children could find themselves empowered where inter-professional differences emerged from the assessment. For instance, when the professional judgement of Alistair's educational psychologist was challenged by a psychologist working for the social services department, the former gave a high profile to Alistair's own account of his difficulties and needs because his account supported his interpretation of Alistair's needs. Although there was no strong evidence in this study of children exploiting professional differences to manipulate outcomes there would clearly be scope for such a strategy in some cases.

NEGOTIATIONS BETWEEN CHILDREN AND PROFESSIONALS: THE ROLE OF CHILDREN'S METAPERCEPTIONS

The difficulty experienced by professionals in their attempts to give children a voice in their own assessments can, in part, stem from the form of children's resistance to what they see as the disempowering consequences of an assessment. In this lies the importance of children's metaperceptions of the assessment because it is on the basis of these that strategies of resistance will be developed. Yet unfamiliarity with the assessment procedures, the formal power embedded in professional roles and the interpersonal power of 'experts' in one-to-one situations make it difficult for children to enact successful strategies. In particular, children may be susceptible to the disempowering consequences of their misperceptions of the process and of professional roles, even where those professionals are fully committed to involving children in their assessments. However, in saying this one must bear in mind how these misperceptions may themselves be the product of the system of assessment and of the broader social context in which the assessment takes place.

Observations of the assessment procedures and subsequent interviews with children revealed evidence of how children's perceptions and misperceptions of the assessment, its purpose and the roles of the professionals involved in carrying it out, influenced the behaviour of children during the assessment. For instance, when Stephen was removed from an off-site behavioural unit by his parents, after they had rejected an educational psychologist's recommendation of residential special education, he commented that, whereas up to that point his behaviour had been 'bad', 'now I can start being good'. For Stephen his removal from the unit meant that the adults around him now had changed expectations about his ability to control the behaviour which, up to that point had, in his eyes, been excused precisely because those adults perceived there to be 'special' reasons for its occurrence. This was a case of a child feeling empowered by his perception of the assessment outcome, even though it was a misperception of what the professionals in this case had actually been arguing for. His strategy of conforming to adult expectations of his behaviour as 'normal' rather than 'maladjusted' gave him the power to determine his own future. Other cases, however, illustrated how such misperceptions might disempower the child during a special needs assessment.

There were a number of very clear occasions when professionals were unaware of what children understood to be happening in the assessment. These resulted, in part, from the absence of any real attempt to listen to children's accounts, but they can also be seen as arising from the particular relationship between children and professionals in the assessment process.

A child's compliance with the assessment and its outcome might imply acceptance of the label attached by professionals or other adults. Certainly there were children in the sample who responded to the label of 'behavioural difficulties' by behaving badly on the grounds that 'I must be naughty'. Children's responses to questioning by professionals could sometimes also be seen as reflecting the child's 'learned helplessness' in the face of a process over which they perceived themselves to have no control.

The concept of learned helplessness originated in the work of Seligman (1975), who argued that the experience of helplessness undermines the motivation to respond and can lead to symptoms of emotional disturbance and anxiety. Where children did not offer psychologists alternative accounts of their difficulties to those put forward by their teachers or parents this might have been a reflection of their sense of powerlessness in the decision-making process. On the other hand, the appropriateness of the concept of learned helplessness to an understanding of what is going on in these interactions depends upon assumptions about the meaning of children's responses which may not be justified. Children in the sample were concerned that what they said in interviews with professionals might be used against them. In some cases children felt unable to articulate responses to the accounts of their behaviour presented by adults involved in their assessments. The apparent learned helplessness of these children could be interpreted as a coping strategy motivated by a rejection of the identities being constructed for them by the assessment, together with recognition that they lacked the power to confront these labels by means of participation in the procedures.

The way in which children perceive the role and power of professionals can lead to breakdowns in communication. The assumptions made by professionals when interpreting children's behaviour may also lead to the rationality of that behaviour being questioned. Breakdowns in communication may, in these circumstances, be taken by professionals as observable evidence of a child's learning difficulties or emotional maladjustment. This can be illustrated by events during Peter's assessment. Peter's silence and lack of co-operation when questioned by a psychologist about his wishes was interpreted as supporting evidence previously obtained from personality testing, which suggested that Peter's behaviour might be explained in terms of a personality disorder. However, when interviewed by a researcher who, as Peter was aware, had no role in his assessment, Peter confided that he was frightened about being taken away from his family and that it was 'The psychologist [who] wants to send me away'. Peter's anxiety about the role of the psychologist led him to distrust the psychologist's motives and, therefore, he was unwilling to co-operate with the professionals' assessment. Thus, whilst the psychologist interpreted Peter's behaviour during interview as a reflection of his personality disorder, Peter's own account of his behaviour during this interview was given in terms of his expectations of the assessment itself. Peter's anxiety about the role of the professionals in the assessment caused him to distrust them and to question their motives in seeking information from him. His refusal to co-operate with the professionals can, therefore, be understood in terms of a distinction drawn by Tammivaara and Enright (1986) between questioning that is perceived by children to be 'controlling' and that perceived to be 'deferential'. Whereas in the former questioning appears to be directed towards securing responses which fit into a pre-established interpretative framework, the latter is concerned not only with showing respect towards the child's point of view but is also intended to empower the child in the decision-making process regarding his or her own needs and interests.

In his interview with Peter the psychologist interpreted Peter's behaviour in terms of a clinical diagnosis of his state of mind, a diagnosis unrelated to Peter's own views about the assessment and the circumstances leading up to its commencement. In failing to recognize and acknowledge the authenticity of Peter's perspective on the assessment process the psychologist was unaware of the possible significance of Peter's behaviour as a strategy for subverting the assessment procedures and what was perceived by him to be its likely outcome. The lack of any theoretical framework from which to explore Peter's perspective as an authentic perspective in its own right inhibited the psychologist's evaluation of the information he obtained from interviews with him. Ironically, in the absence of any framework for understanding the strategic character of Peter's behaviour, Peter's resistance to the assessment and its consequences actually contributed to the construction of his 'deviant' identity.

CONCLUSION

It is clear that many psychologists and teachers would like to involve children in decision-making and would welcome initiatives leading to this being undertaken systematically within their LEAs and schools. In practice, however, the advice of the Department of Education and Science (DES 1989a) has generally been left at the door of individual professionals. Perhaps not surprisingly professionals are concerned about the difficulties of turning good intentions into good practice. Whether this will change under the guidance of the new Code of Practice issued by the DFE (1994) remains to be seen.

The genuine concerns that many professionals have about how to encourage the participation of children as partners in the assessment and decision-making processes may tie in with a deeper concern amongst those professionals; namely, that their work in respect of formal assessments under the 1981 Act is frequently reactive. The possibilities available to professionals to take account of the perspectives of children may be undermined by the crisis that has initiated the assessment. The decision to initiate the assessment, because it reflects a particular view of the child's needs which then becomes the starting point for subsequent negotiations, may itself implicitly lead to the disempowerment of the child. Thus, it may not be 'poor practice' that leads to the child's perspective being disregarded but rather the demands of a complex situation in which the needs of competing clients (school, parents, LEA and child) may determine the extent to which the child's perspective *is allowed to be relevant.* In the absence of clear policy on the role of the child in the assessment, and procedures being established to empower the child, the conflicts of interest that permeate an assessment will continue to inhibit the development of frameworks for partnership with children, denying them a voice.

The formal procedures of the assessment, including interviews involving children, are social events in which the distribution of status and power between participants is culturally embedded in the interactions that occur. Inequalities in the distribution of power between professionals, parents and children may make contradictory any involvement in the assessment procedures by the latter. The child's lack of control over these procedures, together with the cultural imbalance in status between child and adult participants, may lead to a consensus in which the child's involvement serves merely to legitimate decisions taken by adults.

The negotiation of a consensus may be seen as a struggle for power in which resistance is an element of the negotiation. Some forms of resistance may result in a negotiated consensus which reinforces the distribution of power between social groups (for example, between children and professionals or between children and their families). The outcome of children's resistance, therefore, may be a consensual redefinition of their oppositional interests in ways that reinforce their disempowerment as a subordinate social group.

Chapter 7

Professionalism and power
The construction of special educational needs

The need, generated by modern forms of economic and social organization, for a centralized system of control and discipline for the young has increasingly led to the state playing an important role in childcare. This centralization of child-care responsibilities is directly mirrored in the growth of professional groups expressing a claim to expert knowledge in respect of children's needs. From psychologists to speech therapists, from educational social workers to teachers of English as a second language, the application of expert knowledge to the care and control of children has been a major phenomenon of the twentieth century. Yet the diversity of professional claims to child-care responsibilities belies a picture of state intervention drawn solely in terms of an homogeneous system of state control.

The concept of 'control' is complex and multi-dimensional. We live in an increasingly child-centred society in which concern about the needs of children is a dominant theme in the culture of our daily lives. Despite this, or perhaps because of it, there is evidence that ever larger numbers of children are being identified as having 'special' needs of one sort or another. Amongst these children are those seen as disadvantaged by social and environmental conditions, those believed to be ill-equipped physically or mentally to cope with the complexities of modern living, and those whom because of abuse or neglect have been psychologically damaged. Humanitarian justifications for increasing the amount of professional involvement in the care and control of children are not necessarily linked to any overarching design to impose or maintain social order. However, the legitimacy of different professional interests (within as well as between professional groups) depends very much upon the belief that childcare policies are based upon humanitarian principles.

This chapter seeks to explore the nature of professional roles within the modern state and, in particular, focuses upon the implications of recent policy changes which, it is alleged, have resulted in the deskilling of educational professionals. Starting from a discussion of the development and structure of professionalism it will be argued that, despite the challenge to professional autonomy that is implicit in the neo-liberal reforms of the 1980s and 1990s, professionals continue to pursue their interests within the administrative bureaucracy of the state. The contestation between different interests which takes place within the institutions of the state has far-reaching consequences for professional practice and for the way in which the needs of service users are identified and addressed.

THE STRUCTURE OF PROFESSIONALISM

The expansion of professional groups, legitimized by what Larson (1977) has called 'the culture of professionalism', has been a significant feature of the development of the modern capitalist state in the late twentieth century. This culture includes the specialized training and language characteristic of each professional group, together with claims to expert practice which separates professionals from their clients. The early sociology of professional groups assumed that these groups were by definition homogenous, composed of members with shared identities, values and interests. On the basis of this assumption those characteristics or attributes were sought after which would distinguish them from other, non-professional, occupational groups. It was argued that a definition could then be made in terms of those unique attributes that had been identified. This is the approach found in the work of Carr-Saunders and Wilson (1962), for instance. A significant break with this model was made by Johnson (1972), who criticized what had become known as 'trait theories' on the grounds that such theories assumed a functional value to all sections of society for professional activity. According to Johnson, this assumption disguised the relationships of power that created and maintained professional authority. Implicit in the concept of power are the notions that conflict actually or potentially exists between different interests in society, and that power is exercised in order to create or control conflict in pursuit of interests.

Johnson's analysis of professional groups was based on a theoretical perspective that defined professional groups by forms of control rather than in terms of something inherent in the occupation itself. Thus, he maintained that 'professionalism is a historically specific process which some occupations have undergone at a particular time, rather than a process which certain occupations may always be expected to undergo because of their own "essential qualities" ' (Johnson 1972: 45). What is important to an understanding of the growth of professional groups is the way in which the power structures of these occupations have developed. Three types of structure are identified by Johnson as defining professional activity at different historical stages: collegiate, patronage and mediation.

In the collegiate profession power is exercised by members of the occupation itself. They define the processes and outcomes of their work, who shall be admitted to membership and who shall be their clients. There may be an internal hierarchy within the profession so that all members do not necessarily have equal power, but the profession is characterized by the image of internal unity which it presents to the outside world. Examples of professions controlled by a collegiate structure are those of medicine and law.

In the second form of professional structure identified by Johnson power is exercised as an outcome of negotiations between members of an occupation and those who pay directly for its services. Examples given by Johnson of this patronage structure include the professions of architecture and accountancy, where practice is defined by contractual obligations between the professional and client.

The third form of structure identified by Johnson is the mediated profession. Within this structure the relationship between the occupation and the users of the services which it provides is mediated through a third party with its own interests in the nature and distribution of services which are to be provided. The mediator may be another profession or agency but in advanced capitalist societies it is most commonly the state. It occurs where the state comes between professional and client to define the client's needs and the ways in which those needs are to be met. Through this process of mediation certain occupational groups are incorporated into the decision-making machinery of government. Where the state, rather than self-regulating professional bodies, is principally responsible for determining the manner in which occupational services are to be carried out, state mediation fosters the dependence of professionals on the state. However, it also has the effect of encouraging different interests within the occupation because the state itself is composed of many different, frequently conflicting, interests. In consequence, the growth of a common professional identity is inhibited. The processes involved are dynamic, and therefore definitions of professionalism that focus on specific attributes fail to take into account both the control that is exerted over professional groups and the strategies by which members of occupational groups seek to empower themselves.

PROFESSIONS AND THE STATE

The role of the state in relation to the professions is in fact two fold. On the one hand, the state acts as mediator between the different professions and their clients, defining who those clients should be and how they should be helped. On the other hand, the state is itself the client, because professional agencies exist to provide services which are deemed to be 'in the public good', a concept synonymous with the needs of the state. Whilst inter-professional rivalry has historically been a feature of the procedures relating to special education decision-making (Pritchard 1963; Tomlinson 1982), this conflict has not taken place independently from the changing role of professional groups. Indeed, it can only be adequately understood within the context of the assimilation of professionals into the state bureaucracy.

As the state became increasingly concerned with defining the needs of its citizens new professions, like that of educational psychology, have challenged the authority of more traditionally organized professions. The early pre-eminence of the medical profession in special education is evident from the discourse of handicap which has been dominant throughout much of the twentieth century. However, the medical profession, with its collegiate systems of control, was only partially absorbed into the administrative bureaucracy of the state and consequently was not fully responsive to the needs of a rapidly expanding system of state selective education which demanded quick and easy procedures for the classification of children into groups ranging from the most academically able to the 'subnormal'. Later, the discourse of special education was modified to include the concept of 'psychological deficit' (both in the form of mild/moderate learning difficulties and behavioural difficulties) reflecting the growing importance of the profession of educational psychology. The new authority of educational psychologists had its origins in the policies of selection and control upon which the proposals for educational expansion in the inter-war years were built – see, for instance, the *Report of the Consultative Committee on the Primary School* (the Hadlow Report), 1931, and the *Report of the Consultative Committee on Secondary Education* (the Spens Report), 1938. More recently, educational administrators have extended their professional role through the control they now exercise over the allocation of resources.

The power of different professions to define their clients depends upon their ability to negotiate aspects of their role with the state. The state is ultimately the mediator between the different professional interests competing for 'ownership' of the same clients. In addition to mediating between these interests, the state is also the client of its professional agencies, with interests of its own. To some extent the relationship between the power of professionals as service providers over service users and the origin of this power in the role of professionals as agents of the state is disguised by the humanitarian ideology of professionalism.

This ideology is not a complete sham, and it is important to avoid ascribing some form of metaphysical existence to the state, particularly one which represents the state as having interests independently of the social groups by which it is constituted. The state has interests only in so far as the goals transmitted through its institutions express the interests of particular groups. Predominant amongst these interests are the interests of the most powerful social groups. Those institutions of the state which have a social welfare role, such as the education system, also serve to reinforce the legitimacy of the social structure through the services provided to benefit less powerful social groups. However, the state is not simply a vehicle for crudely reproducing social order by domination and force; it is itself a site of contention for power between different social groups. In particular, dominant social groups contend for and negotiate their power, both with each other and with subordinate social groups, through the agencies of the state (including its welfare and educational institutions). The *consensus* between groups with different social and economic interests is formed through *conflict* taking place within the social institutions of society. The state, therefore, is a site for the conflict of different and opposing interests but its function is also to represent the forms of consensus that are constantly being negotiated and renegotiated.

This characterization of the state has been central to recent theoretical debates about the role of the state in social life (Apple 1982; Aronowitz and Giroux 1985). It suggests that subordinate social groups are actively contending for power within the institutions of the state, exerting influence (though not control) over its institutions and policies. Apple (1982: 29) puts it as follows: 'hegemony isn't an already accomplished social fact but a process in which dominant groups and classes manage to win the active consensus over whom they rule'. Moreover, 'to maintain its own legitimacy the state needs gradually but continuously to integrate many of the interests of allied and even opposing groups under its banner' (Apple 1982: 30).

The social power of professionals within the apparatus of the modern state has been widely documented. Bowles and Gintis (1976), for instance, maintained that through the institutional role of schooling in capitalist society teachers reproduce those forms of consciousness, dispositions and values that maintain the form of social relationships necessary for the 'translation of labour into profit'. However, this rather one-dimensional representation of the role of educational professionals and the outcomes of their actions fails to recognize the possibility that the meanings attached to their own roles by different professionals may have quite different consequences for their professional practice. By abstracting the concept of professionalism from the historical specificity of the real-world relationship between professionals and their clients, and from the forms of control by which these relationships are constructed, of the ways in which contradictions within the roles of professionals in modern societies may actually create conditions under which they are able to act independently of the interests of dominant groups within the state are ignored. At the heart of this abstraction is an inadequate account of the contradictory role of professional bureaucracies within the modern state. It is interesting, and not a little ironic, that the thrust of the neo-liberal critique of professionalism has been the claim that professions are self-interest groups whose functioning within the administrative bureaucracies of the state, far from reproducing the institutionalized interests of the dominant social class, has undermined those interests.

The power of an occupational group within the state apparatus at any given time will indeed, in large part, be dependent upon the correspondence of its activities with the interests of dominant groups. However, where the professional interests of an occupational group are themselves threatened by the changing interests of dominant groups, and/or by changes in the balance of power between conflicting interests represented within the state apparatus, strategies may be adopted and alliances forged by the group or by sub-groups and individuals in an effort to preserve their power in opposition to, as well as within, the state bureaucracy. This can be seen, for instance, in the recent decision of the British Psychological Society to create a new category of membership with 'chartered status' designed not only to enhance and protect the interests of its clinicians but also to assert its own authority as a professional body with the right to define who shall be admitted to membership and to exercise controls over the processes and outcomes of psychologists' work – in effect, to counterpoise elements of a collegiate system of control to the system of state mediation. This move, far from bringing the occupation into conflict with the state, actually anticipates the possible consequences of neo-liberal reforms and the changed relationship between service providers and service users implicit in the 'privatization' of welfare. In contrast to this move towards internal professional autonomy in alliance with, but distinct from, the state, the way power is exercised by members of professional groups may also be subject to a much broader range of influences, some of which may conflict quite sharply with the interests of socially dominant groups (for instance, in relation to disputes over public expenditure on special educational services). A good example of this can be seen where psychologists are actively involved in work to support action groups such as the British Dyslexia Association, the Down's Syndrome Association, Parent Network, and so on.

The lack of homogeneity within professional groups which derive their power from their role within the state bureaucracy reflects the diversity of interests within the state itself. As the relationship between the state and service users has been reconstructed under the influence of neo-liberalism, seeds have been sown which encourage greater fragmentation of professional roles and responsibilities as different occupational groups compete for ownership of clients. On the other hand, members of those occupational groups may adopt strategies aimed at retaining power over their professional practice with clients (clients who includes the state and its institutions such as schools as well as the more traditional service users with special needs) by their contestation for control over the definition of client needs and the nature and extent of service provision. Alternatively, new alliances may be forged both with other occupational groups whose professional role within the state is threatened and with subordinate social groups whose interests are neither represented within the state nor compatible with those who wield power through it. Consideration of the dynamic, as opposed to deterministic, relationship between different social interests will allow a better understanding of professional roles and of the contradictory pressures to which they are subject as intermediaries between dominant and subordinate social groups. It will also allow a clearer picture to be obtained of the circumstances in which professionals may either advance the interests of subordinate groups or enforce the consensus upon which the powerlessness of these groups is predicated.

THE NEGOTIATION OF PROFESSIONAL ROLES THROUGH THE IDENTIFICATION OF SPECIAL EDUCATIONAL NEEDS

The introduction of a national curriculum to be followed in all state schools has removed from teachers the control they once had over what is taught in schools (as well as how much and when), centralizing power over the curriculum and education policy in the hands of government. The procedures for nationally assessing the learning of all children at 'key stages' of their schooling, together with the publication of each school's results, has forced teachers to be accountable for the delivery of a curriculum over which they may perceive themselves to have little control.

The deskilling of mainstream teachers in these respects can be seen as forming the context for teacher deprofessionalization as structural changes in the organization and control of education increasingly bring challenges to the professional autonomy of teachers from those outside the profession. Thus, devolution of financial control from LEAs to schools has created and empowered a new managerial bureaucracy within those schools, whose concerns rest primarily with competitiveness and budgetary control rather than with educational philosophies and goals. The rise of post-modernist thinking in education (Bauman 1992; Harvey 1989) has seen the downgrading of the ideology of professionalism and its replacement with a new managerial ideology which aims to debunk the claims of professionals to expertise based on the rational application of knowledge by subjecting them to competitive trial by market forces. Whereas the influence of teacher professionalism within LEAs once gave teachers direct access to policy-making mechanisms that could counterbalance national policy initiatives, the decline in the power of LEAs has undermined the efforts of teachers to influence recent policy changes.

In consequence of these changes in their professional responsibilities the deskilling of teachers may take place at two levels. In the first place, the professional status of teachers is undermined by the loss of skill and autonomy, the increase of stress, the increase of supervision and the creation of reskilled specialisms (Lawn and Ozga 1988). Second, the loss of professional autonomy and control which teachers feel themselves to have suffered may lead to responsibility for 'problem' children being shifted into the hands of outside 'experts', including educational psychologists and the staff of specialist schools. The apparent willingness of teachers to identify large numbers of children whose needs cannot be met in their mainstream schools might be understood as reflecting this process of deskilling. The appeal to outside 'experts', such as psychologists, may indicate a narrowing of the skills to which teachers are able to lay claim. Where schools are under pressure to adopt pupil selection and financial policies that maximize their competitiveness in the market-place, classroom teachers may respond to pressures from their own management teams by refusing to accept responsibility for severely disruptive pupils, with the consequence that teaching is routinized in terms of the administration of the 'normal' curriculum for 'normal' children.

However, as a theoretical framework for the analysis of recent changes in teachers' professional roles, the deskilling thesis may obscure ways in which teachers act in defence of particular conceptions of their professional roles. The assumption underlying the deskilling thesis is that the teacher's role is determined by external forces that construct that role in the labour market. However, teachers may also be seen as determining agents interacting with those external forces (the national curriculum, government policy and so on), not simply passively responding to them. Lawn (1988) has suggested that teachers may resist attempts to deskill their work by adopting strategies aimed at negotiating their role as 'skilful' in the day-to-day work relations of their school. Such strategies are not without their contradictions, but an exploration of these contradictions may provide some useful insights into the processes by which professional identities, together with the social identities of their clients, are constructed.

DISRUPTIVE OR DISTURBED?

Foucault (1967), in his study of the history of insanity, argued that madness was once accepted as a part of normal society because it was believed that those who were afflicted expressed visionary insights into the experience of everyday life. It came to be seen as a disease at precisely that moment when it threatened emerging conceptions of rationality. Rationality was to provide the ideological justification for a new social order whilst opposition to that order was marginalized as an 'absurdity'. According to Foucault the concept of insanity was primarily given meaning by the different social and political functions it served in different historical periods.

Although it is improbable that teachers ever saw 'disturbed' children as visionaries, there is, none the less, an analogy that can be drawn between the development of the modern concept of madness and the distinction that teachers draw between disturbed and disruptive behaviour in children. Galloway et al. (1982), in their study of schools and disruptive pupils, pointed out that although the concept of maladjustment was frequently invoked to remove disruptive pupils from ordinary lessons it was unclear what behaviours this concept actually referred to. Although it was not a category recognized by the most widely used classification systems in child psychiatry, it did provide a label under which special education could be provided when a school was no longer able or willing to tolerate a child's behaviour. In labelling behaviour as disturbed rather than disruptive an implicit claim is made about the irrationality of that behaviour, and therefore that a child suffering from an *emotional* disturbance needs specialist treatment that cannot be provided by a mainstream school. The supposed irrationality of the behaviour legitimizes the removal of the child into special education but it also legitimizes the school's failure to effect changes in the child's behaviour.

Observations made of meetings between teachers and psychologists during my own research on the assessment of children identified as having emotional and behavioural difficulties suggested that teachers' needs, and their expectations of an assessment, are often explicitly recognized. This is illustrated by the comments of one head teacher made during a discussion with her school's educational psychologist:

> What is important is that the teachers get some support for Bryan in the classroom. We should have had the extra support before now. . . . We can't be expected to teach him without extra help . . . something will have to be done. The child has suffered and the teachers have suffered.

The expectation behind many referrals is illustrated in another school's report to the LEA:

> Difficulties at high school include: threats to others, confrontation with staff, general class disruption and finally an incident with a girl that finally led to his exclusion. . . . His home circumstances are unsuitable as they do not give the right type of support necessary for him to achieve a stable emotional state. I feel a new environment in terms of school and home would be of benefit.

However, the ways in which these expectations may affect the contributions teachers make to the assessment have been relatively unexplored. The educational report that a school provides for the LEA constitutes the formal part of its contribution to the assessment, whilst an informal part is frequently found in teachers' negotiations with educational psychologists and their LEAs regarding the nature of the 'problem' and how it should be dealt with. Once a decision to request an assessment had been made by teachers two themes can be identified as consistently arising from both the formal reports and informal negotiations making up teachers' contribution to the assessment.

First, when teachers identify children as having emotional and behavioural difficulties they frequently believe the behaviour of these children to be qualitatively different from the behaviour of 'ordinary' children. One teacher in the study was typical of many when she observed that 'I've got a very bad class this year. A lot of difficult boys. But Damien isn't like them. With them it's because they get no discipline. With Damien that's not it. He's just strange.' Despite conceptual weaknesses and a lack of empirical foundation, the distinction between 'disturbed' and 'disruptive' behaviour was one that was drawn by teachers of sixteen of the twenty-nine children in the study. A common characteristic of the accounts given by teachers in these cases was their reference to causal factors for the child's behaviour over which they, as teachers, had no control: 'He's crackers, absolutely crackers. He talks to himself and answers himself. He walks around school making weird physical gestures. Psychologically the kid is disturbed. He needs help.'

The notion of the child's culpability, or lack of culpability, for behaviour is important, because where it could be shown that a child did not exercise rational control over his or her behaviour teachers made the assumption that they could not be held responsible for that child's behaviour in the classroom. In other words, when teachers requested an assessment of a child who, they claimed, had emotional and behavioural difficulties, implicit in this request was a parallel claim that the child's unacceptable behaviour was not, and could not be, influenced by practices within the classroom or school.

Interestingly, a similar view is expressed in the Elton Report on Discipline in Schools (DES 1989b: paragraph 6:29). Because the report was principally concerned with 'disruptive' pupils, it was necessary to distinguish these children from those with 'emotional and behavioural difficulties'. The latter were said by the Elton Committee to be in evidence when children show 'severe and persistent behavioural problems as a result of emotional, psychological and neurological disturbance [such] that their needs cannot be met in mainstream schools'. In part this definition is clearly tautological. It is claimed that an emotional, psychological and neurological disturbance is evident where there is a severe and persistent behaviour problem. Likewise, a behaviour problem is judged to be severe and persistent when it is caused by an emotional, psychological and neurological disturbance. On the other hand, it is also revealing in just the same way as is the distinction teachers make between disruptive and disturbed behaviour, because it suggests that a criterion to be used in distinguishing disturbed from disruptive behaviour is that the needs of children belonging to the former category 'cannot be met in mainstream schools'. The Elton Committee recognized that

> it is sometimes difficult to distinguish between ordinary bad behaviour and disturbed behaviour, *but the distinction has to be made*. Judgements must be made by teachers, educational psychologists and other professionals in individual cases.
>
> (DES 1989b: paragraph 6:30) (italics added)

In exercising this judgement, teachers in my own study identified children as disruptive rather than disturbed where they believed they could manage with the resources ordinarily available to them in their schools. Where it was felt that children's behaviour demanded the allocation of resources and facilities not normally available within mainstream schools they were then likely to be identified as having 'emotional problems'. This emphasis upon resources reflects very accurately the criteria adopted by the 1981 Education Act to define special educational needs.

Thus, the second theme to emerge from the study of teachers' contributions to the assessment was that the distinction they drew between qualitatively different types of behaviour had its origins in the resources perceived to be available to their schools. None the less, despite emanating from a resource-led model of needs, the distinction between 'disruptive' and 'disturbed' is one that is likely to have significant consequences for subsequent perceptions of individual child identities. This point may be illustrated by the comments of a primary class teacher who had once worked in a residential ebd school but whose experiences there had led her to become a 'committed integrationalist':

> I was quite concerned by the difficulties presented by Tony. In attempting to teach him I would have maintained that classroom behaviour problems ultimately revolved round questions of classroom management. As teachers we are concerned with what we can affect and that is the child's learning and behaviour in the classroom. Behaviour management comes down to teacher skill. However, Tony undermined my self-confidence as a teacher because I had not succeeded in making changes in his class behaviour. I felt emotionally drained after a session with Tony and I felt my failure to cope effectively with Tony was undermining the ethos of my classroom.

Eventually, in her report to the LEA, this teacher wrote:

> We have recently been allocated a classroom assistant for 9 hours a week to meet the complex needs of Tony. I strongly feel that Tony's needs will not be met in this way. Tony's disturbed behaviour patterns require full time attention. . . . I have twenty-seven other children in my class.

These different skills were not seen as being higher order skills. Indeed, it was common for teachers to claim that if they had the opportunity to teach on a one-to-one basis they could easily cope educationally with an emotionally disturbed child. Whilst they often added that emotionally disturbed children needed specialist counselling, this was seen as separate from their educational needs; as teachers they would be able to cope if they were not responsible for twenty-five or thirty other children.

This focus upon resources for children with learning difficulties reflects a dilemma recognized by the authors of the Warnock Report:

> On the one hand we are aware that any kind of special resource or service for such children runs the risk of emphasising the idea of their separateness. . . on the other hand unless an obligation is placed on local education authorities to provide for the special needs of such children there is a danger that their requirement for specialist resources will be inadequately met.
>
> (DES 1978: 45)

By defining children's needs in terms of resources those needs are individualized, inhibiting consideration of the context in which they occur, a context which includes the expectations and needs of those who request and carry out the assessment. For instance, head teachers in the study were particularly concerned about the negative effects on staff morale and on other children in their schools brought about by the presence of children whose behaviour was disturbing.

In consequence of there being no formal acknowledgement of the needs of other participants in the assessment process, once the procedures are invoked teachers may feel that their own needs can only be expressed in terms of the child's needs. Yet this creates a discourse which assumes a focus on the child whilst inhibiting any meaningful discussion of circumstances within the school which might affect a child's behaviour. In this way the 1981 procedures for identifying and assessing children with special educational needs may themselves contribute to a deskilling of teachers by discouraging reflexivity on practice (Armstrong *et al.* 1993).

THE NEGOTIATION OF TEACHERS' ROLES

It is important to bear in mind that teachers do not necessarily form a group whose perception of professional interests is entirely homogeneous, even within the same school. Negotiations between teachers over the decision to refer a child for assessment may reflect differing professional interests as well as differing perceptions of a child's needs. This was evident in negotiations taking place between teachers in one high school that was visited. Here, teachers with different areas of responsibility within the school revealed themselves to be conscious of different areas of concern. Simon's form tutor wanted 'some intervention type strategy' from the psychologist: 'It was very important to get an official, an alternative view. We certainly found the psychologist useful in the past and we wanted to get her perspective.'

Bernard, head of special needs, was mindful of differences within the school's staff over what should be done about Simon. He was also conscious that if children with special needs were to be helped in the school it was necessary for him to retain the confidence of other members of staff. Thus, he could not hold out for a child where the majority of staff felt it to be a hopeless case:

> There are differences between members of staff about what should be done. On the one side there are those who want to get rid of Simon, and on the other those who feel the school is in need of expert advice on his handling. I felt the referral might be the first step towards getting him put away, but he was referred as a last resort. This was not the option I preferred but I felt that the balance of opinion on the staff favoured this option. It's a question of whether you see it as a child deficit model or a systems model. On balance there were more members of staff who saw it in terms of a child deficit model.

Simon's head of year, although not expressing any strong views about Simon's needs, none the less was very conscious of the implications of not initiating the statementing procedures:

> To be honest I don't know what Simon's needs are but if we are going to request statementing to be commenced it is important to initiate the process before the end of a child's third year. After that nobody really wants to know. Other children become priorities for resources.

Negotiations over referral decisions may, as in this case, focus upon broader, political considerations relating to the allocation of resources within an authority rather than solely upon how individuals perceive their own roles and skills as teachers. Therefore the decision to refer a child for assessment does not imply a perception on the part of teachers making the referral that they lack appropriate skills. Indeed, the decision by an LEA to initiate an assessment may reflect the success of teacher negotiations as the latter seek to define their role in terms of their skills with more able, higher-status children.

Once a decision has been taken to refer a child for assessment, this decision will be a major factor affecting future developments. Henceforward, those who are involved in the formal assessment must take account of the needs of those who are disturbed by the child's behaviour, difficulties with learning, physical or sensory disabilities. Moreover, the decision to refer a child for assessment is usually made in anticipation of a particular outcome – either the removal of a child from the school or the acquisition of additional resources. In consequence, an assessment under the 1981 Act is often seen by teachers as a bureaucratic mechanism for effecting that outcome. Actions taken by the school prior to and during the assessment may be intended to reinforce and explicate the expected outcome. The referrals of ten children for formal assessments were made at the same time as they were permanently or indefinitely excluded from school. In a further seven cases children were given periods of temporary exclusion whilst the assessment was actually in progress. In each case it was made clear that the exclusion resulted from the head teacher's perception of the inter-relationship between the child's needs, the needs of teachers with classroom responsibilities for the child, and the needs of other children in the school. After one child in the study had been excluded, his head teacher argued that

> I felt we had our quota of disturbed children. . . . It was a shame he had to go home where the problems were but there was a lot of disruption in the class and other children would be affected. The class was a different place after he had gone. . . . The fact that he has been removed from school is a plus for us, the other children and the staff. We hate excluding children but our hands are tied.

In turn, this resulted in quite specific expectations about the outcome of the assessment, often that the child would not return to the school. Educational psychologists were generally very sympathetic to the position teachers were in but recognized that 'an exclusion shuts doors in terms of possible recommendations. I think the head teacher was quite aware of that but at the end of the day they do it because they've tried everything else.'

NEGOTIATING CONTROL: TEACHER PERSPECTIVES ON ASSESSMENT

A strong case can be made that there are inconsistencies between the 1981 Education Act and the earlier Warnock Report. By tying resources to individual 'statemented' children the 1981 Act forces teachers to conceptualize children's needs in terms of deficits rather than focusing upon and supporting effective teaching interventions. The effect of this can be to deskill mainstream teachers in their work with children with special educational needs as emphasis is placed upon identification rather than intervention. The Act does invest teachers with considerable professional responsibilities for the identification of those children. It is usually teachers who initiate 'statementing' procedures. Moreover, they are required to contribute educational advice as part of the assessment. What teachers lack, however, is the power to make decisions about the allocation of additional resources to meet needs once they have been identified. This power lies with the local authority and involves quite different issues from those involved in the professional assessment of children's needs.

In so far as teachers provide professional advice to their LEAs their role is similar to that of educational psychologists. The two professions fulfil complementary functions in the assessment of special needs. Ostensibly, the prime responsibility of educational psychologists under the 1981 Education Act is also one of providing their LEAs with independent expert advice on children's special educational needs. Yet, by linking resources to individual children, the 1981 Education Act has perpetuated a conceptualization of needs in terms of available resources. The assessment of needs, therefore, can become a matter of matching needs to resources rather than resources to needs. This has important implications for professional advisers. The formal distinction between the advisory role of professionals and the administrative role of LEA officers may become blurred as professionals respond to the 'realities' of resource availability within an authority to maximize the effectiveness of their professional intervention on behalf of clients. Thus, in practice, psychologists may often fulfil an important bureaucratic function relating to the distribution of resources within an LEA. Either directly or indirectly, depending on the procedures operating within different authorities, psychologists become the gatekeepers to resources, or at least are seen as such by teachers.

Yet the role of the psychologist is ambiguous. Other clients, including teachers, parents and children may have interests that are very different from those of the authority, but each may have legitimate expectations of the psychologist's intervention. Consequently, the bureaucratization of the psychologist's professional role as gatekeeper, or perceived gatekeeper, to resources may result in psychologists becoming the focus of conflict between the competing interests of different clients as each attempts to negotiate a particular outcome of the assessment (Armstrong and Galloway 1992a). In these negotiations some clients are clearly more powerful than others. The well-documented inequality of power between professionals and parents (Armstrong and Galloway 1992b; Swann 1987; Tomlinson 1981; Wood 1988), and between professionals and children (Armstrong *et al.* 1993) may be contrasted with a perception of shared power frequently held by different professionals in their negotiations with one another (Armstrong *et al.* 1991). These latter negotiations are likely to take place on the basis that each party does have a more or less equal power to influence events. Yet, teacher perceptions of psychologists' roles may operate in significant ways to set the agenda for the assessment process. This can be seen, for instance, in Robin's assessment, where his teachers' perceptions of their own needs significantly affected the outcome of the psychologist's assessment even though in the expert judgement of the latter Robin did not have special educational needs.

Although senior staff at Robin's school were confident that they had the skills and resources to meet his needs, his parents were concerned about his behaviour and persuaded them to seek a psychologist's opinion. It later emerged that Robin had been referred to the school psychological service when at primary school and on that occasion his head teacher had described Robin as 'a very disturbed child'. However, when the family moved home and Robin changed schools, the psychologist decided not to initiate a formal assessment under provisions in the 1981 Education Act because at his new school the 'disturbing' forms of behaviour previously reported had not 'resurfaced'. On this latest occasion, in the absence of any great concern on the part of the school, the psychologist once again thought it unnecessary to recommend a formal assessment of Robin's needs. He did, however, arrange for the LEA's behavioural support service to monitor Robin's progress in school.

Following this recommendation concern was expressed by some of Robin's teachers. This focused on three anxieties. First, there was a growing concern over the suggestion made by Robin's mother that he was 'psychiatrically disturbed'. In particular, they were concerned about the history of psychological involvement and began to doubt their future ability to cope with a boy who had been identified as a 'psychological case'. Second, this anxiety led to an increasing awareness of Robin's behaviour in school. Thus one teacher commented that 'there are signs that he might flip. He's become a bit more fidgety. There are signs that he's bubbling.' Other teachers expressed concern over reports that Robin had been heard talking to himself. Third, Robin's teachers also began to doubt the adequacy of the support that would be available from the behavioural support service if Robin was indeed a 'disturbed' child. These concerns led to a request for statementing procedures to be initiated after all. It was now argued by the school that this would be appropriate even if it did no more than formally specify Robin's need for extra help from the behavioural support service.

Robin's teachers put pressure on the educational psychologist and the LEA to initiate a formal assessment of his special educational needs with a view to the issuing of a formal statement of those needs. In response to this request, the psychologist and staff from the behavioural support service entered into discussions with Robin's teachers, and eventually agreed to recommend a formal assessment under the Act. The negotiations between teachers and psychologist in this case illustrate Armstrong and Galloway's (1992b) claim that clinical criteria are not the principal criteria used by psychologists in assessments under the 1981 Education Act. The negotiations taking place between participants during the assessment may have a far more significant effect on its outcome. Although Robin's statement of special educational needs, when issued, did no more than formally endorse the existing arrangements, the school, none the less, saw this as a legal document which would in some unspecified way impose an obligation on the LEA to make alternative arrangements for Robin if his behaviour were to deteriorate. From the perspective of Robin's teachers, far from resulting in a transfer of their skills to the psychologist the assessment had concluded with a successful negotiation of their own needs that gave recognition to the skills embedded in their professional role. Whilst the management of classroom behaviour was seen as comprising one of those skills, dealing with the 'disturbed' child whose behaviour, because of its irrationality, posed particular difficulties in the context of an ordinary classroom was not seen as falling within the professional responsibilities of these teachers. Robin's teachers, as was the case with others in this study, believed that in a one-to-one or small-group setting they could effectively meet the educational needs of a disturbed child. However, for them this was not the issue, because (1) the education of the disturbed child could not be managed effectively within the context and resources of the ordinary classroom; (2) the presence of a disturbed child in the ordinary classroom seriously impeded the learning of all children in that classroom; and, (3) their skills were principally related to the 'higher status' concerns of educating 'ordinary' children rather than to teaching children with special needs. By insisting on alternative provision for Robin if his behaviour was to deteriorate, his teachers were legitimizing their own view of their professional role.

CONCLUSION

The power of educational professionals over their clients is derived from their administrative role within the bureaucracy of the state, not from their professional expertise in its own right. Ultimately, it is the state that defines clients' needs and how these needs are to be met. Therefore, the interests of professional groups are tied up not only with the state but with *the relationship between the state and client groups.* Because the state incorporates different interests in a dynamic and dialectical relationship to one another, professionals are less constrained by common professional interests than would be the case if client needs were defined by the professional agencies themselves. However, as government policy has led to professionals increasingly playing an explicitly administrative role (whether that be in the form of educational psychologists servicing statements of special educational needs or of teachers administering a national curriculum), the contradictions between professional services performed on behalf of clients and bureaucratic functions performed on behalf of the state have become more sharply defined. On the one hand, these constraints limit the freedom of professional agencies to define the parameters of their own activities, whilst, on the other, they lead to a more fragmented perception of professional interest linked to concerns from within these occupational groups over the deskilling of their work. This has the consequence of bringing professionals into conflict with one another as they attempt to negotiate a new consensus about their respective professional roles (and by implication a consensus about the needs of particular children).

In this chapter it has been argued that government policy, far from valuing schools which are successful with children with social, emotional and behavioural difficulties, actually focuses attention on the achievements of more able children. Resulting from this policy, more pupils are being identified as having special educational needs and, following assessment and statementing, these children are likely to be educated in segregated settings. However, research has identified how strategies are employed by teachers in an attempt to negotiate enhancements in the status of their professional role. One way in which this has been seen to occur is through the emphasis given to successful work with 'normal' children, which may include children whose behaviour is 'disruptive' but not those identified as 'disturbed'.

The identification of a child as having special educational needs may ensure that the professional competence of those with responsibility for that child in the mainstream schools is not brought into question. In particular, where a child is identified as 'emotionally disturbed' teachers may view this as less threatening to perceptions of their competence as teachers than might be the case had the child merely been labelled 'disruptive'. Whereas the latter might raise questions about the teacher's classroom management skills, the former assumes that the child's personality and emotional or family history make it difficult for him or her to respond rationally in 'normal' classroom situations. Where teachers' expectations of a formal assessment under the 1981 Act are that a child's emotional and behavioural difficulties will (or should) be formally recognized by the LEA, research suggests how this outcome may be seen by teachers to legitimize their decision to involve a psychologist or other 'outside' expert without at the same time threatening their own professional status.

Far from undermining the professional responsibilities of teachers, the assessment procedures may actually provide mainstream teachers with the opportunity to enter into negotiations with other educational professionals about the nature of their teaching role, resulting in a redefinition of their expertise in terms of higher-status skills associated with teaching more able children. The removal of the disturbed child is legitimized in terms of this conceptualization of the teacher's role. In turn, this child-centred focus can constrain the type of intervention available to school psychologists who may, in these circumstances, find it difficult to develop a theoretical model for examining how the needs of all participants are constructed in, or affected by, the school context. As HMI (1990) commented, work with individual children remains central to the role of educational psychologists and this largely reflects the strong pressures placed upon them to respond to the way teachers initially define the problem.

Research on the assessment of emotional and behavioural difficulties has shown that teachers on some occasions at least ask for children to be seen by psychologists in order to establish or negotiate a particular definition of their professional skill as teachers. These teachers see themselves making a crucial contribution to the identification of children's special educational needs, whilst psychologists and other outside experts may be seen primarily as gatekeeper to resources. Where this was so, the recommendations made by these 'experts' will be influenced by the strategies adopted by teachers. Thus, in seventeen of the twenty-nine cases in the study of assessments related to emotional and behavioural difficulties, children were excluded from school either immediately prior to or in the course of a formal assessment. In these cases, even when a psychologist considered that a child's needs *could* be met in that school, or in an alternative mainstream school, the chances of implementing this option were greatly reduced. Similarly, as in one child's (Robin's) case, some teachers saw statementing as necessary, even though there were no specific resource implications over and above those that could be made available without a statement. The teachers' perceptions of Robin's difficulties underwent a change as they became more aware of the possible implications for themselves of decisions taken about him. Discussions between the school and the psychologist at this stage focused on the negotiation of the professional role of the teachers.

At one level this may be seen as evidence of teachers being deskilled since outside 'experts' increasingly become responsible for an area of work previously under the control of teachers (the identification of the needs of disturbing children and the planning of specialist programmes for these children). However, evidence has been presented in this chapter which suggests teachers may counter measures that tend to deprofession-alize their role by adopting strategies aimed at renegotiating their role with 'ordinary' children as 'skilful'. It has been argued that the referral to outside experts of children who present difficult or disturbing behaviour in the classroom may constitute just such a strategy. Responsibility for the execution of programmes for children identified as having special needs would become the task of teachers in special schools and units (or specialist teachers in the mainstream). Traditionally, these specialists in behaviour problems have been regarded in mainstream schools as having lower status than those teachers working with highly motivated, academi-cally orientated pupils. Where a statement of special educational needs is provided this is likely to be seen by teachers, not as evidence of a lack of skill on their part, but as the outcome of a successful negotiation of those professional skills.

Chapter 8

Partnership and professional identities

Finch (1984) has argued that education systems have increasingly provided explanations for social and economic inequalities in terms which account for and legitimize that inequality. The education system may fulfil the function of providing a vehicle for advancement within a meritocracy, yet it also serves as a tool for defusing political dissent by promoting the notion that the privileged deserve to be there. When, during times of economic recession, the opportunities for social mobility through education decrease, schools are likely to come under increasing pressure. On the one hand, the contraction of opportunities fuels the competition between schools for the role of gatekeeper to this scarce commodity. On the other hand, the ability of schools to defuse dissent is threatened by economic decline and/or restructuring. The presence of increasing numbers of children in school who perceive education as a poor investment and who see no benefits to be gained from conforming to the values the system promotes may make the socializing role of the school *towards all its children* more difficult.

The humanitarian concerns which led (following the Warnock Report and the 1981 Education Act) to the needs of up to 20 per cent of the school population being recognized as 'special' may actually be, as Tomlinson (1985: 157) argues, 'an ideological rationalisation which obfuscates the educational, political and economic needs actually served by the expansion.' Thus, the concept of special education itself inhibits any genuine discussion of the needs and interests actually being served by the expansion of special education. Those who adopt a humanitarian perspective on special needs 'still have to explain why a whole sub-section of special education has developed and expanded, which is backed by legal enforcement and caters largely for the children of the manual working class' (Tomlinson 1985: 164).

The conceptualization of educational failure, disturbing behaviour and disablement in terms of personal deficits, for which a humanitarian concern is appropriate, serves to marginalize and contain opposition to structural changes in society. The legacy of the humanitarian conceptualization of 'needs', divorced as it is from an analysis of the social power of those who are affected directly and indirectly by it, may be legitimation of the disempowerment of the 'needy' by denying them the opportunity to negotiate a definition of their own needs in terms of their political and social origins.

Professionals working with children who are experiencing difficulties within educational contexts may feel constrained to define the problem in terms of the difficulties a child presents to others despite being sensitive to the influence of wider social and political contexts. When a child is referred for assessment it is unlikely to be the result solely of a disinterested concern to identify a child's special educational needs. Other reasons for the referral might include the expectations the child's teachers have of the assessment outcome, the acquisition of resources or the removal of a troublesome child. Evidence from the research discussed in this book suggests that educational professionals do not and *cannot* assess a child's needs without also taking into account and responding to the legitimate expectations of other participants with interests in the outcome of particular assessments. Psychologists, for instance, may feel constrained to negotiate solutions which are acceptable to the schools for whom they are advisers, to their LEA employers and to the parents of children who are the subject of assessment. These constraints reflect some of the deeper ambiguities about the relationship between professionals as both service providers and members of the state's administrative bureaucracy, on the one hand, and service users, on the other hand.

The concept of 'consensus' is central to an understanding of the role played by the modern state in the reproduction of social relations. The idea that power is determined by economic control alone has been rejected here in favour of a more subtle conception of power as emanating from the consent of those over whom power is exercised but under circumstances in which there is a continual renegotiation of the limits of that power. Moral authority is not necessarily conceded to the form taken by the consensus at any particular time by those who are constrained by it (though such authority may be claimed and advocated by those whose interests it advances). The authority and power which underpins the form of any consensus will, in all likelihood, continue to be contested; this happened in many of the cases which have been discussed here. Indeed, the resistance of subordinate social groups is itself an expression of the power these groups have to determine their own lives at specific moments. The process of contention and negotiation creates conditions in which opposition and resistance are endemic to the process of social reproduction itself.

The precise nature of the consensus is not predetermined by existing forms of social relations. The domination of powerful groups, however, is derived from their success in constantly renegotiating the consensus in ways which accommodate the needs of subordinate groups, whilst at the same time reproducing their relative powerlessness and dependency by the way in which those needs are defined. The character of this renegotiation does not preclude conflict nor the use of state power by dominant groups to impose their interests by force. Their power, however, ultimately depends upon the creation of needs which are perceived by the needy to arise from their own failings or from circumstances over which they can exert no control.

The ideologies of welfarism and of neo-liberalism are but two sides of the same coin. This does not mean that these ideologies are identical. The struggle between different social groups which is reflected in these different forms of consensus is far from insignificant. The policies of the welfare state on the one hand represent improvements in the conditions of life for subordinate social groups, achieved through their own struggle, whilst on the other hand they represent the continuing domination of more powerful social groups who have conceded no more than a redefinition of the consensus upon which legitimization of their power is founded. The rise of neo-liberalism, grounded in the restructuring and globalization of capitalism and established through the protracted political, industrial and social struggles of the last twenty-five years, has led to a redefinition of the consensus upon which the power of dominant social groups is based. The expansion of the welfare state during a time (and as a direct consequence) of world-wide economic restructuring has led those groups exercising greatest power within the state to resolve the crisis by putting the long-term interests of capital before those of welfare, challenging the legitimacy of state welfare services (Gough 1979; Offe 1984). The new 'consensus' implicitly separates individual needs from any social context and therefore rejects social responsibility both for their creation and for their consequences (the corollary of this being the idealization of individual wealth which, ideologically freed from the social context of its production, denies any legitimacy to social ownership and control). The atomization of needs and the consequent fragmentation of social responsibility reflects the disintegration of economic protectionism and welfare capitalism worldwide (events in Eastern Europe providing a spectacular example of this process) and has been fundamental to the restructuring of capitalism in the late twentieth century.

PARTNERSHIP, POWER AND PROFESSIONAL INTERESTS

Under the influence of social welfarism the Warnock Report (DES 1978) advocated a redefinition of special educational needs (later incorporated into Section 1(1) of the 1981 Education Act), which emphasized the social character of needs and appropriateness of meeting them through a model of social responsibility. Just as significantly, the Report recommended that social responsibility be taken for meeting the educational needs of a large number of children (18 per cent of the school population) in respect of whom schooling previously had operated merely as a means of social constraint following their academic deselection. Although it was estimated that only 2 per cent of the school population would be likely to have special educational needs so severe that they would require additional resources over and above those normally available within a mainstream school, by introducing a social dimension to the concept of needs it followed that the criteria used to identify those children with special educational needs would necessarily vary from case to case. Warnock's recommendation that special educational needs be demedicalized and procedures introduced for assessing educational needs not only weakened the power of medical professionals *vis-à-vis* that of teachers and psychologists, but it also led to far greater emphasis being placed upon negotiations between professionals in the assessment procedures. Moreover, whatever the interests of the child, the interests of professionals would inevitably become tied to their ability to negotiate definitions of children's needs in terms of their own professional models. The criteria to be used to identify children's needs would vary in each case, depending upon the outcome of negotiations between participants in the assessment. These negotiations would not only lay the basis for interventions with the child but would also inform the consensus which in each case legitimates the dominance of one professional perspective over others and the inequality between professional and parental contributions to the assessment.

Fulcher (1989: 165), in a discussion of the impact of the Warnock Report, has argued that its 'recommendation on statementing procedures endorsed bureaucratic management and effectively *bureaucratised practices*'. In consequence, she argues, the parents-as-partners model only makes sense within the context of an 'entrenched professionalism'. In other words, partnership incorporates parents into the bureaucratic procedures established to service the needs not of children but of the social institutions of the state. Far from allowing parents the means to exercise genuine power in the decision-making procedures of special needs assessments, their involvement serves to facilitate the smooth operation of the bureaucratic procedures themselves.

The deconstruction of this entrenched professionalism in the post-Warnock era by the policies of neo-liberalism has forced professionals into responding to Warnock's model of special educational needs through different, frequently contradictory, models of practice. Professional action may emanate from the self-interest of entrenched professionalism, but as the concept of needs, atomized and individualized through public policy, has been stripped of its social connotations (connotations explicitly emphasized in the definition of special educational needs put forward in the Warnock Report), this has also emphasized the ambiguities that characterize professional roles in today's society. In particular, these ambiguities have encouraged professionals to use the assessment procedures as a forum for negotiating within the institutions of the state over their own power to specify both the scope of their expertise and how the needs of their clients are to be met. The professional practice of educational psychologists provides a good example of how these processes work.

The Department of Education and Science in its advice on the implementation of the 1981 Education Act (DES 1989a) asserted that assessments should be carried out without regard to the type of provision available within the LEA. Yet psychologists, whose contribution to the assessment is pivotal, may encounter pressures that make consideration of the availability of resources difficult to avoid. This can operate entirely at an informal level, as is the case when psychologists perceive their professional credibility with schools and parents to be dependent upon recommendations being made which are meaningful within budgetary and policy constraints operating within their LEA. At a more formal level, educational psychologists may be drawn directly into the decision-making process where they are called upon to provide the LEA with advice on the placement and resource implications of different options (in separate reports which are not circulated to parents because, technically, they are not part of the professional advice sought by the LEA under the 1981 Education Act). In one recent case which received national publicity, the refusal of an educational psychologist to comply with an LEA directive to remove a paragraph in his report (a report subsequently made available to parents), explaining that his assessments for the LEA under the 1981 Education Act required him to advise on children's needs, not to make recommendations as to how those needs should be met, led to his dismissal (Pyke 1990). The consequent ethical and professional dilemmas can seriously affect the ability of the psychologist to represent the interests of any or all of these clients, resulting in highly reactive rather than proactive interventions.

From the perspective of LEAs, which have to juggle competing demands from schools and parents whilst operating within highly pressurized budget constraints, the role the psychologist in an assessment of special educational needs is seen to be one of providing advice which can then be used as the basis for administrative decision-making about the allocation or non-allocation of resources. Parental participation in this process is valuable because it allows the LEA to operate its procedures on the basis of a consensus model. The tensions experienced by psychologists as a result of their responsibilities towards different clients (namely child, parents, schools and LEA) can likewise only be satisfactorily resolved through the development of consensus. Thus, a consensus model of special educational needs is built into the psychologist's professional practice precisely because of the ambiguity of his or her role in the assessment procedures. When consensus is clearly established psychologists are unlikely to experience any role conflict. Where there is an absence of consensus the psychologist becomes involved in the management of conflict by attempting to modify the perceptions of other participants. A compromise is aimed for whereby different participants will see their own needs through decisions taken in respect of the child's special educational needs. It is in this situation, however, that the psychologist is most vulnerable to misperception of parental objectives and wishes.

The consensus model is particularly poor at handling questions relating to the differential distribution of power between different participants. It fails to address the issue of how power is conveyed and perpetuated by the conceptual structures and usage built into the assessment process by the Act. Where these questions and issues are addressed in the practice of individual psychologists it may force rejection of the consensus model upon them, at least in particular cases. Where this occurs, however, it will bring individual psychologists into conflict with one or other individual or group of participants. Conflict with powerful interest groups create threats to professional autonomy and the possibility of psychologists themselves being disempowered. This may create conditions which allow a psychologist to identify with the broader social interests which underpin the actions of their clients.

Yet the form of control to which professionals, as members of the state bureaucracy, are subject (that is, the mediation of the state between professionals and service users to define client needs) also means that it can be unclear to professionals who their client is. Is it the state, which in addition to the competing interests of dominant social groups includes different layers of professional and administrative bureaucracy? Or is it those whom the state has defined as service users? This lack of clarity is not necessarily reproduced in the subjective understanding of professionals in their day-to-day practice. From this perspective the service user (for example, the child) is invariably seen as the principal or even sole client. Yet, regardless of the humanitarian principles which psychologists adopt when viewing their own action, this subjective understanding of who the client is can itself serve to veil the range of conflicting interests which influence their practice in ways which operate to disempower not only the service user but the professional as well.

It is certainly the case that the 1981 legislation on the assessment of children's special educational needs increased the rights of parents to involvement in the decision-making process. Despite this, parents still feel unable to exercise their rights in any meaningful way. The power embedded in professional roles may often place parents at a disadvantage in their interactions with professionals. To say this is not to question the integrity or 'good faith' of professionals working with parents in the assessment of children's special educational needs. It is far too simplistic, and in most cases plainly wrong, to suggest that professionals deliberately manipulate parents into accepting decisions the latter do not want to make. The interactions between professionals and parents, together with the wider contexts within which those interactions take place, are far more complicated, and their implications far more contradictory, than is suggested by an account based solely upon the power that professionals have over parents.

Professionals do have their own interests in the outcomes of assessments, and these are related to the ways in which the professional identities of those involved in assessments are perceived both by themselves and by others. It is clear that professionals adopt strategies in pursuit of objectives related to these interests. However, this does not mean that a conspiracy theory of professional activity is theoretically appropriate or adequate to explain interactions taking place during an assessment. In addition to what professionals may perceive as their own personal values, their professional ethic and their professional interests, they are also subject to quite contradictory pressures from their different clients. Psychologists must have regard for the legitimate concerns of the schools for whom they provide advice as well as for the concerns of children and their parents. Teachers must not only have regard for the different and sometimes conflicting needs of all children in their classes but respond also to the increasingly centralized systems of control which the state exerts over professional life in schools. Although these different pressures may combine to impose severe constraints on professional action they also present challenges to the homogeneity of professional practice. They highlight the fact that professionals are forced to make choices in their practice which sit uneasily with an ethic of professional service governed solely by the interests of children.

Teachers and psychologists alike forcefully complain that too much of their time is spent on the bureaucratic procedures for obtaining additional support for children with special educational needs. There is considerable frustration over the limits these procedures place on their opportunities for actually working in meaningful partnerships with these children and their parents. Statementing is widely recognized by the professionals involved to be a bureaucratic procedure for managing resources. In practice, these procedures have also provided a site for the management of conflicting interests. However, the opportunities available to professionals for empowering parents, by providing independent information and advice, are inhibited by constraints imposed on them by their responsibility and accountability towards different, often more powerful, clients.

In the changed political and economic climate of the 1980s and 1990s, characterized by the assertion of an ideology of individual responsibility for individual need and a policy of public expenditure reduction, special needs have become ever more a matter for negotiation between those involved in the assessment, with the consequence that the professional assessment of children's needs can no longer be adequately understood solely in terms of the application of specialized systems of knowledge. This has had a considerable effect on the role of professionals carrying out assessments. The contradiction inherent in Warnock's social welfare model of needs has been starkly exposed by this.

It is not simply the case that the social welfare model upon which Warnock is based is out of step with the economic and social individualism of the 1980s and 1990s, though it most certainly is so. The real contradiction lies in the fact that, despite recommending the abolition of categories of handicap in favour of more socially orientated criteria, the definition of special educational needs proposed in the Report ultimately fails to free itself from a conception based on individual deficits. Although the social origin of needs is acknowledged and the importance of a social response accepted, the concept of special educational needs confines this response to adapting the individual to the system or modifying the system to take account of individual differences. The educational system may be efficient or inefficient in its management of individual needs, but it is presumed that the state is ideologically neutral in its relationship with its citizens. Untrammelled by considerations of power and social interests, the authors of the Warnock Report assumed the benevolence of the state towards the needs of its citizenry to be logically derived from the application of rational principles of efficient management.

Warnock's conception of multi-disciplinary assessment, involving the child's parents as equal partners with professionals, rests upon an assumption that needs are *identified*, disregarding how those needs are *constructed* through the assessment process itself. Despite the efforts of the Warnock Committee to promote an understanding of individual needs in their social context, in practice precisely because of the social character of needs, the procedures used to identify children's needs focus also upon negotiations about professional roles and the operation of systems of control. The significance of the inter-relationship between social interests, negotiation and decision-making is entirely overlooked by the model of parent–professional partnership proposed by the Warnock Report and contained in the 1981 Education Act. The model is founded naïvely upon a two-fold assumption: first, that the only interests professionals and parents have in the outcome of an assessment are the interests of the child; second, that the determination of special educational needs will be arrived at solely as a consequence of the application of expert judgement (including the expert judgement of parents exercised through their partnership with professionals). In reality there may be many factors which affect the decision to initiate an assessment and the course it takes thereafter, not all of which are necessarily related to the needs of the child being assessed. In addition, the form and relevance of expertise acquires its meaning, not from the relationship between professional and child, but rather from the relationship between the state and the different social groups which constitute the society in which we live.

CONCLUSION

This book set out to subject the concept of partnership in special educational decision-making to critical scrutiny. Inevitably much of the discussion has focused upon power. It has been argued that despite the formal position of parents and, to a lesser extent, children as partners with professionals, the experience parents and children have of these procedures continues to expose the deep cracks which run through the model of partnership. Moreover, it is misleading to assume that the interests of children and their parents are necessarily coincidental. As was seen in Chapter 5 this is often far from the case.

The ambiguity of professional roles, in particular, has been highlighted as problematic. On the one hand, many professionals cling to an ethic of service derived from beliefs about the independence of their professional judgement founded in the rational application of expert knowledge. On the other hand, the administrative bureaucracy of the state mediates between professional and clients both to define the needs of the latter and to define the parameters of intervention by the former. Increasingly, as the independence of professional judgement has been brought into question by dominant political groups within the state, these ambiguities have led to conflict between professionals and service users. This arises, in part, because the scope for professional action, not legitimated by the state, is limited. Within these constraints professionals, like children and their parents, are able to negotiate not only their own interests but also the interests of service users. Thus it is possible for professionals, in particular circumstances, to work effectively in the interests of children. Yet, significantly, more insidious constraints upon professional independence are located, as with the constraints upon children and their parents, in the meaning and use of the concept of 'needs' in our society. It is through the construction of needs in the interests of the powerful that power is sustained. The construction of children's needs and of parents' needs cannot be adequately understood without giving recognition to how the needs of professionals are themselves constructed within the institutions of the state.

For children and their parents the outcome of partnership may, in practice, amount to disempowerment by consensus. In these circumstances, the most effective partnership may be that which is forged through the strength of collective action outside the structures of the state and against the imposition of needs by the state. For those professionals who seek to identify with the interests of their clients it is necessary to go beyond the concept of needs to examine the use and legitimation of power in their practice. This may lead some, at least, to challenge their role within the administrative bureaucracy of the state and to forge genuine partnerships with children and their parents through which education becomes a true means of personal and social empowerment for those who today are disenfranchized by 'needs'.

Bibliography

Abrams, M. and Rose, R. (1960) *Must Labour Lose?* London: Penguin.

Acland, H. (1980) 'Research as stage management: the case of the Plowden Committee', in M. Bulmer (ed.) *Social Research and Royal Commissions*, London: George Allen & Unwin.

Adler, M., Petch, A. and Tweedie, J. (1989) *Parental Choice and Education Policy*, Edinburgh: Edinburgh University Press.

Apple, M. W. (1982) *Education and Power*, Boston: Routledge & Kegan Paul.

Aries, P. (1962) *Centuries of Childhood*, London: Cape.

Armstrong, D. and Galloway, D. (1992a) 'On being a client: conflicting perspectives on assessment', in T. Booth, W. Swann, M. Masterton and P. Potts (eds) *Policies for Diversity in Education*, London: Routledge/Open University.

—— (1992b) 'Who is the child psychologist's client? Responsibilities and options for psychologists in educational settings', *Association for Child Psychology and Psychiatry Newsletter*, 14(2): 62–6.

Armstrong, D., Galloway, D. and Tomlinson, S. (1991) 'Decision-making in psychologists' professional interviews', *Educational Psychology in Practice*, 7(2): 82–7.

—— (1993) 'The assessment of special educational needs and the proletarianisation of professionals', *British Journal of Sociology of Education*, 14(4): 399–408.

Aronowitz, S. and Giroux, H. (1985) *Education under Siege: The Conservative, Liberal and Radical Debate over Schooling*, London: Routledge & Kegan Paul.

Association of Educational Psychologists (1992) *Members' Handbook*, AEP.

Audit Commission (1992) *Getting in on the Act. Provision for Pupils with Special Educational Needs: The National Picture*, London: HMSO.

Bannister, A., Barrett, K. and Shearer, E. (eds) (1990) *Listening to Children: The Professional Response to Hearing the Abused Child*, London: Longman.

Barton, L. and Meighan, R. (1979) *Schools, Pupils and Deviance*, Nafferton, Driffield: Nafferton Books.

Bauman, Z. (1992) *Intimations of Postmodernity*, London: Routledge.

Bernstein, B. (1962) 'Social class and linguistic development', in A. H. Halsey, J. Floud and A. C. Anderson (eds) *Education, Economy and Society*, London: Free Press.

Blumer, H. (1962) 'Society as symbolic interaction', in A. M. Rose (ed.) *Human Behavior and Social Processes*, Boston: Houghton Mifflin.

—— (1969) *Symbolic Interactionism*, Englewood Cliffs, NJ: Prentice-Hall.

Booth, T. and Statham, J. (eds) (1982) *The Nature of Special Education*, Milton Keynes: Open University Press.

Bourdieu, P. and Passeron, J. C. (1977) *Reproduction in Education, Society and Culture*, London: Sage.

Bowles, S. and Gintis, H. (1976) *Schooling in Capitalist America: Educational Reform and the Contradiction of Economic Life*, New York: Basic Books.

Burgess, R. (1984) *In the Field: An Introduction to Field Research*, London: George Allen & Unwin.

Butler-Sloss, E. (1988) *Report of the Inquiry into Child Abuse in Cleveland in 1987*, London: HMSO.

Callaghan, J. (1976) 'Speech by the Prime Minister', the Rt. Hon. James Callaghan, MP, at a foundation-stone laying ceremony at Ruskin College, Oxford, on 18 Oct. (press release).

Carr-Saunders, A. M. and Wilson, P. A. (1962) *The Professions*, Oxford: Oxford University Press.

Central Advisory Council for Education (CACE) (1967) *Children and Their Primary Schools* (The Plowden Report), London: HMSO.

Charon, J. M. (1979) *Symbolic Interactionism: An Introduction, An Interpretation, An Integration*, Englewood Cliffs, NJ: Prentice-Hall.

Chaudhury, A. (1986) *Annual Report of the Advisory Centre for Education*, London: ACE.

Cooper, P. (1989) 'Respite relationships and re-signification: a study of the effects of residential schooling on pupils with emotional and behavioural difficulties, with particular reference to the pupils' perspective', unpublished PhD thesis, University of Birmingham.

Cox, A. and Rutter, M. (1976) 'Diagnostic appraisal and interviewing', in M. Rutter and L. Hersov (eds) *Child Psychiatry: Modern Approaches*, Oxford: Blackwell.

Cox, C., Douglas-Home, J., Marks, J., Norcross, L. and Scruton, R. (1986) *Whose Schools?* London: The Hillgate Group.

Croll, P. and Moses, D. (1985) *One in Five: The Assessment and Incidence of Special Educational Needs*, London: Routledge.

Davie, R. (1991) *Listen to the Child*, Vernon Wall Lecture, Annual Conference of the Education Section of the British Psychological Society.

Davie, R. and Galloway, D. (eds) (forthcoming) *Listening to Children*, David Fulton.

Department for Education (1992) *Choice and Diversity. A New Framework for Schools*, London: HMSO.

—— (1994) *Code of Practice on the Identification and Assessment of Special Educational Needs*, London: HMSO.

Department of Education and Science (DES) (1975) *The Discovery of Children Requiring Special Education and the Assessment of their Needs* (Circular 2/75), London: DES.

—— (1978) *Special Educational Needs* (The Warnock Report), London: HMSO.

—— (1983) *Assessments and Statements of Special Educational Needs* (Circular 1/83), London: DES.

—— (1989a) *Assessments and Statements of Special Educational Needs: Proce-*

dures within the Education, Health and Social Services (Circular 22/89), London: DES.

—— (1989b) *Discipline in Schools* (The Elton Report), London: HMSO.

Department of Health and Social Security (1976) *Fit for the Future* (The Court Report), London: HMSO.

Douglas, J. W. B. (1964) *Home and School*, London: McGibbon & Kee.

Dyson, S. (1986) 'Professionals, mentally handicapped children and confidential files', *Disability, Handicap and Society*, 1(1): 73–87.

—— (1987) 'Reasons for assessment: rhetoric and reality in the assessment of children with disabilities', in T. Booth and W. Swann (eds) *Including Children with Disabilities*, Milton Keynes: Open University Press.

Echols, F. E., McPherson, A. and Williams, J. D. (1990) 'Parental Choice in Scotland', mimeograph, Centre for Educational Sociology, University of Edinburgh.

Finch, J. (1984) *Education as Social Policy*, London: Longman.

Ford, J., Mongon, D. and Whelan, M. (1982) *Special Education and Social Control: Invisible Disasters*, London: Routledge & Kegan Paul.

Foucault, M. (1967) *Madness and Civilization: A History of Insanity in the Age of Reason*, London: Tavistock.

Fox Harding, L. (1991) *Perspectives in Child Care Policy*, London: Longman.

Fraser, E. (1959) *Home Environment and the School*, London: University of London Press.

Freeman, M. D. A. (1987) 'Taking children's rights seriously', *Children and Society*, 1(4): 299–319.

—— (1990) 'Listening to children and representing them – a lawyer's view', in A. Bannister, K. Barrett and E. Shearer (eds) *Listening to Children: The Professional Response to Hearing the Abused Child*, London: Longman.

Fulcher, G. (1989) *Disabling Policies: A Comparative Approach to Educational Policy and Disability*, London: Falmer.

Galloway, D. (1985a) *Schools Pupils and Special Educational Needs*, London: Croom Helm.

—— (1985b) *Schools and Persistent Absentees*, London: Pergamon.

Galloway, D., Ball, T., Blomfield, D. and Seyd, R. (1982) *Schools and Disruptive Pupils*, London: Longman.

Galloway, D. and Goodwin, C. (1979) *Educating Slow Learning and Maladjusted Children: Integration or Segregation?* London: Longman.

—— (1987) *The Education of Disturbing Children: Pupils with Learning and Adjustment Difficulties*, London: Longman.

Gersch. I. S. (1987) 'Involving pupils in their own assessment', in T. Bowers (ed.) *Special Educational Needs and Human Resource Management*, London: Croom Helm.

—— (1992) 'Pupil involvement in assessment', in T. Cline (ed.) *Assessment and Special Educational Needs: International Perspectives*, London: Routledge.

Gersch, I. S. and Cutting, M. C. (1985) 'The child's report', *Educational Psychology in Practice*, 1: 63–6.

Gersch, I. S., Holgate, A. and Sigston, A. (1993) 'Valuing the child's perspective: a revised student report and other practical perspectives', *Educational Psychology in Practice*, 9(1): 36–45.

Gersch, I. S. and Noble, J. (1991) 'A systems project involving students and staff in a secondary school', *Educational Psychology in Practice*, 7(3) 140–7.

Gillick vs *West Norfolk and Wisbech Area Health Authority* (1986) 1 FLR 224.

Giroux, H. (1983) *Theory and Resistance in Education: a Pedagogy for the Opposition*, New York: Heinemann.

Goacher, B., Evans, J., Welton, J. and Wedell, K. (1988) *Policy and Provision for Special Educational Needs: Implementing the 1981 Education Act*, London: Cassell.

Goffman, E. (1959) *The Presentation of Self in Everyday Life*, New York: Doubleday.

—— (1968) *Stigma: Notes on the Management of Spoiled Identities*, London: Penguin.

Goldthorpe, J., Lockwood, D., Beckhefer, F. and Platt, J. (1968) *The Affluent Worker in the Class Structure*, Cambridge: Cambridge University Press.

Gough, I. (1979) *The Political Economy of Welfare*, London: Macmillan.

Hannam, C. (1975) *Parents and Mentally Handicapped Children*, London: Penguin.

Hargreaves, D. H. (1967) *Social Relationships in a Secondary School*, London: Routledge & Kegan Paul.

Harvey, D. (1989) *The Condition of Postmodernity: An Enquiry into the Origins of Cultural Change*, Oxford: Blackwell.

Her Majesty's Inspectors of Schools (HMI) (1990) *Educational Psychology Services in England 1988–1989*, London: DES.

Houghton, S., Wheldall, K. and Merrett, F. (1988) 'Classroom behaviour problems which secondary school teachers say they find most troublesome', *British Educational Research Journal*, 14: 297–312.

House of Commons (1987) *Special Educational Needs: Implementation of the Education Act 1981*, Third Report from the House of Commons Education, Science and Arts Committee, London: HMSO.

Jackson, B. and Marsden, D. (1962) *Education and the Working Class*, London: Routledge & Kegan Paul.

Johnson, T. J. (1972) *Professions and Power*, London: Macmillan.

Kirp, D. L. (1983) 'Professionalism as a policy choice: British special education in comparative perspective', in J. B. Chambers and W. T. Hartman (eds) *Special Education Policies: Their History, Implementation and Finance*, Philadelphia: Temple University Press.

Kuhn, M. H. (1962) 'The interview and the professional relationship', in A. M. Rose (ed.) *Human Behavior and Social Processes*, Boston: Houghton Mifflin.

Lacey, C. (1970) *Hightown Grammar: The School as a Social System*, Manchester: Manchester University Press.

Larson, M. S. (1977) *The Rise of Professionalism – A Sociological Analysis*, Berkeley: University of California Press.

Lawn, M. (1988) 'Skill in schoolwork: work relations in the primary school', in J. Ozga (ed.) *Schoolwork: Approaches to the Labour Process of Teaching*, Milton Keynes: Open University Press.

Lawn, M. and Ozga, J. (1988) 'The educational worker? A reassessment of teachers', in J. Ozga (ed.) *Schoolwork: Approaches to the Labour Process of Teaching*, Milton Keynes: Open University Press.

Mead, G. H. (1934) *Mind, Self and Society*, Chicago: University of Chicago Press.

Ministry of Education (1945) *Handicapped Pupils and School Health Service Regulations* (Statutory Rules and Orders, no. 1076), London: HMSO.
—— (1959) *The Handicapped Pupils and Special Schools Regulations* (Statutory Instruments no. 365), London: HMSO.
Mittler, P. and Mittler, H. (1982) *Partnership with Parents*, Stratford-upon-Avon: National Council for Special Education.
Moses, D. and Croll, P. (1987) 'Parents as partners or problems?' *Disability, Handicap and Society*, 2: 75–84.
Offe, C. (1984) *Contradictions of the Welfare State*, London: Hutchinson.
Oliver, M. (1988) 'The social and political context of educational policy: the case of special needs', in L. Barton (ed.) *The Politics of Special Educational Needs*, London: Falmer.
Paquette, J. (1991) *Social Purpose and Schooling: Alternatives, Agendas and Issues*, London: Falmer.
Pollock, L. (1983) *Forgotten Children: Parent–Child Relations from 1500–1900*, Cambridge: Cambridge University Press.
Pritchard, D. G. (1963) *Education and the Handicapped 1760–1960*, London: Routledge & Kegan Paul.
Pyke, N. (1990) 'Psychologist wins damages for sacking', *Times Educational Supplement*, 20 July, p. 1.
Rehal, A. (1989) 'Involving Asian parents in the statementing procedure – the way forward', *Educational Psychology in Practice*, 4: 189–97.
Report of the Consultative Committee on the Primary School (the Hadlow Report) (1931), London: HMSO.
Report of the Consultative Committee on Secondary Education (the Spens Report) (1938), London: HMSO.
Riddell, S., Dyer, S. and Thomson, G. (1990) 'Parents, professionals and social welfare models: the implementation of the Education (Scotland) Act 1981', *European Journal of Special Needs Education*, 5(2): 96–110.
Rosenbaum, M. and Newell, P. (1991) *Taking Children Seriously: A Proposal for a Children's Rights Commissioner*, London: Calouste Gulbenkian Foundation.
Rutter, M. and Graham, P. (1968) 'The reliability and validity of the psychiatric assessment of the child: I. Interview with the child', *British Journal of Psychiatry*, 114: 563–79.
Seligman, M. (1975) *Learned Helplessness: On Depression, Development and Death*, San Francisco: Freeman.
Sharron, H. (1985) 'Needs Must', *Times Educational Supplement*, 22 Feb.
Stillman, A. and Maychell, K. (1986) *Choosing Schools: Parents and the 1980 Education Act*, Windsor.
Swann, W. (1984) 'Conflict and control: some observations on parents and the integration of children with special needs', Paper presented to the Annual Conference of the British Psychological Society, Education Section.
—— (1987) 'Statements of intent: an assessment of reality', in T. Booth and W. Swann (eds) *Including Children with Disabilities*, Milton Keynes: Open University Press.
Tammivaara, J. and Enright, D. S. (1986) 'On eliciting information with child informants', *Anthropology and Education Quarterly*, 17: 218–38.
Tomlinson, S. (1981) *Educational Subnormality: A Study in Decision-making*, London: Routledge & Kegan Paul.

Tomlinson, S. (1982) *A Sociology of Special Education*, London: Routledge & Kegan Paul.

—— (1985) 'The expansion of special education', *Oxford Review of Education*, 11: 157–65.

—— (1988) 'Why Johnny can't read: critical theory and special education', *European Journal of Special Needs Education*, 3: 45–58.

Wade, B. and Moore, M. (1993) *Experiencing Special Education*, Milton Keynes: Open University Press.

Walvin, J. (1982) *A Child's World: A Social History of English Childhood 1800–1914*, London: Penguin.

Warnock, M. (1985) 'Teacher teach thyself (The 1985 Dimbleby lecture)', *The Listener*, 28 March, pp. 10–14.

Watzlawick, P., Beavin, J. and Jackson, D. (1967) *Pragmatics of Human Communication: A Study of Interactional Patterns, Pathologies and Paradoxes*, New York: Norton.

Wheldall, K. and Merrett, F. (1988) 'Which classroom behaviours do primary school teachers say they find most troublesome', *Educational Review*, 40: 3–27.

White, P. (1988) 'The new right and parental choice', *Journal of Philosophy of Education*, 22: 195–9.

Willis, P. (1977) *Learning to Labour: How Working Class Kids Get Working Class Jobs*, Farnborough: Saxon House.

Wood, S. (1988) 'Parents: whose partners?', in L. Barton (ed.) *The Politics of Special Educational Needs*, London: Falmer.

Woods, P. (1979) *The Divided School*, London: Routledge & Kegan Paul.

Wright, J. (1989) 'The dishonest statements that protect LEAs – not children', *Childright*, 49: 12–14.

Index